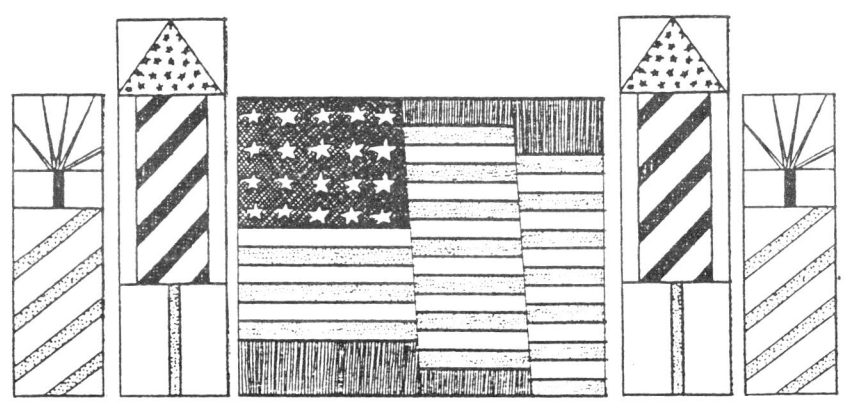

HOLIDAY
PAPER PIECING PATTERNS

by
Shirley Liby

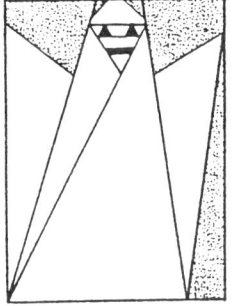
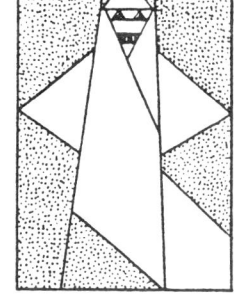

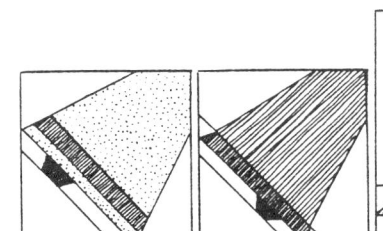
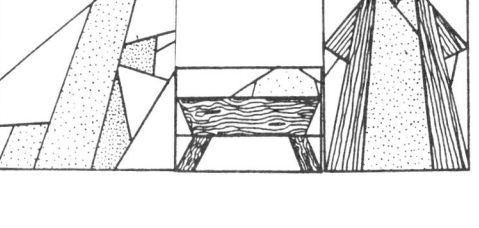
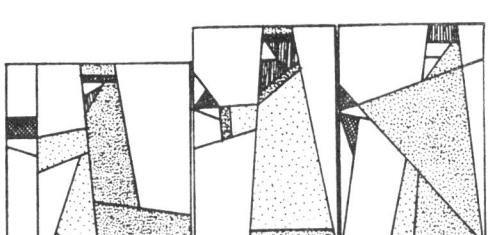

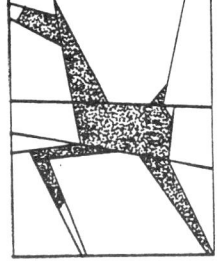
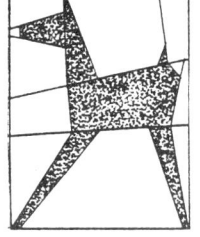
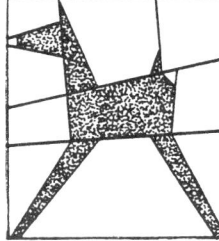
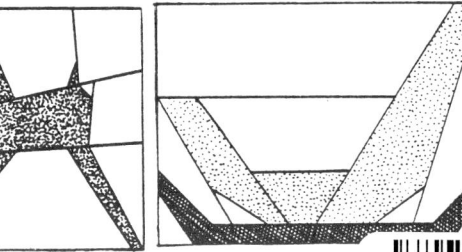
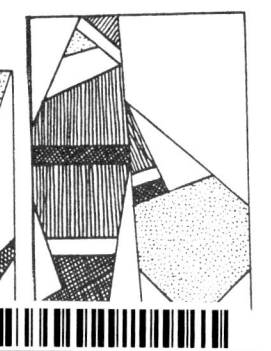

With my heartfelt thanks, I dedicate this book to my students. Over the years I have learned more from them than they have learned from me! Quilters are always generous with their knowledge and insights. I'm so pleased to be associated with such a fine group of people.

SHIRLEY LIBY PUBLICATIONS
2808 West Petty Road
Muncie, IN 47304
(765) 282-9561

For a complete listing of Shirley's other books see the inside and outside back cover.

Hearts & Hands
Creative Resource Distributors
826 E. 49th Street   Indianapolis, IN 46205
(317) 923-7884   Fax (317) 923-8874
Website: http://www.heartshands.com

Many experienced quilters have turned to piecing on a paper
foundation to achieve the wonderful accuracy the technique
offers. It is a quicker way to work, too, because there are no
templates, no marking and cutting of blocks. The technique
is a blessing to beginners as well for they get instant good results.

I have been doing designs for this process for several years now
and have heard from many of my readers asking for holiday
designs that are fun, easy and fast. I have tried to fill the order
with this collection of designs. I hope they are what you all
wanted. Have a great time working your way through the
calendar with HOLIDAY PAPER PIECING PATTERNS.

Shirley Liby

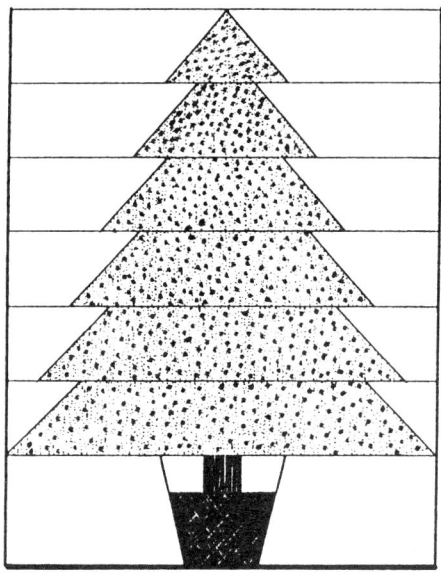   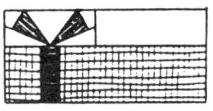  

i

PAPER PIECING INSTRUCTIONS

Here are step-by-step instructions to help you create your first block with this method. You may gnash your teeth and mutter under your breath while you make the first block, but once finished with it you <u>will understand</u>. So take it easy and do one step at a time and you'll do fine. I know that you will find this process fast and easy and you will become as addicted to it as I am!

1. Begin by stitching on all of your pattern lines without thread in your needle. This gives you a raised line of perforations on the back or blank side of your pattern which will help you see and feel the lines on the top side. It might also help to pencil in the piece numbers on the back side for easy reference. As you grow more experienced, you may choose to leave out this step, for it is time consuming. To help you "see" through the paper to place your fabrics, put a small bright light near your sewing machine and hold your pattern in front of it.

2. Place the fabric that you wish to use for piece one over that area on the back of the pattern so that the fabric covers all of piece one and a fourth of an inch all around the edge of the piece as well. The fabric for piece one is face up (wrong side against the paper). Now place the fabric for piece two face down on the fabric for piece one, aligning the edge so that you can sew a seam on the line between piece one and piece two. There should be enough of the second fabric to cover the area of piece 2 and a seam allowance all around it. I usually flip the fabric over at this stage to check for this.

3. Now carefully turn this sandwich of paper and fabrics over so that you can slip it under the presser foot. You can use pins to hold the layers together if you need to but don't place them too close to your sewing line or they can get in your way. At this time you stitch a few stitches before the pattern line, the pattern line and a few stitches beyond the pattern line. I use 12 to 15 stitches per inch when I am paper piecing. If you prefer to backstitch at each end of the pattern line, do so. Remove the fabric and paper combination from the machine and trim the seam you just made to a fourth inch or less.

4. Flip the second fabric over so the right side shows and thumb press it at the seam you just made. Make sure that this fabric covers the area of piece two and has a seam allowance all around it. Now you repeat the process for piece three and the line between piece two and piece three. Work your way through the design, taking each piece in sequence until the block is complete. Pay particular attention that you have sufficient fabric to cover the seam allowance all around the outside edge of the pattern.

5. Now that the block is complete, trim around the pattern on the outside edge (the edge of the seam allowance) and press the finished block with an iron (no steam). I usually complete all of the blocks for my project before I remove the paper foundation. I think it is easier to keep the blocks flat and pressed if the paper remains on them until I am ready to assemble the project. When you are finally ready to put the project together, spend an evening removing the paper. Tear it away in the opposite order from the piecing, last piece first. The paper will come away more easily if you wipe it with a moist sponge before beginning to remove it. Keep tweezers handy for those little stubborn pieces of paper that don't want to come loose. I know

that this seems to be a lot of trouble to go to for a quilt block but, believe me, it is worth it. Remember now that it is PLACE, SEW, TRIM, FLIP, AND PRESS. If you proceed in this order, you will get through the process with ease.

As you work with the designs in this book, you'll find many of them require more than one pattern piece to complete a block. I have tried to arrange the pattern pieces so that it is easy to see how they go together. Pay attention to the numbers and titles on the pattern pieces to help in assembling the right ones together.

As you begin to work with the designs, you will notice that the patterns are mirror images of the pattern illustrations. That is the nature of this technique so always be aware of this phenomenon so you won't be taken by surprise.

Now remember these points and you will get satisfactory results:

*You'll be sewing on the printed side of the paper but your fabric will be on the blank side.

*The pattern pieces are numbered in the order in which you sew them together.

*Each line of stitching holds two pieces of fabric together to the paper backing.

*You need to gather and press your scraps and have them available before you begin.

*You will not need any templates for this process.

*There is no pre-marking or cutting fabric pieces to specific sizes with this technique.

*You have permission to copy any of these patterns for your own personal use.

Now it is time to pick a design and get started on a new project. Have a wonderful time. I have really enjoyed my part in the process and I want you to enjoy yours. Send me your suggestions and snapshots of your successes. I always enjoy hearing from you.

TABLE OF CONTENTS

NATIVITY SCENE

I have been working for some time to create a nativity scene on paper foundation and I have finally finished this one. It would be easy to enlarge to a bigger size by taking the designs to your local copy shop in case you prefer it larger. You can construct the stable, Mary, Joseph and the manger only or you can do the complete scene. It could be done in three panels with the shepherd and sheep on one panel and the wise men on another on either side of the stable. Be sure to select your fabrics with care for they will be of great importance to the overall look of the finished project.

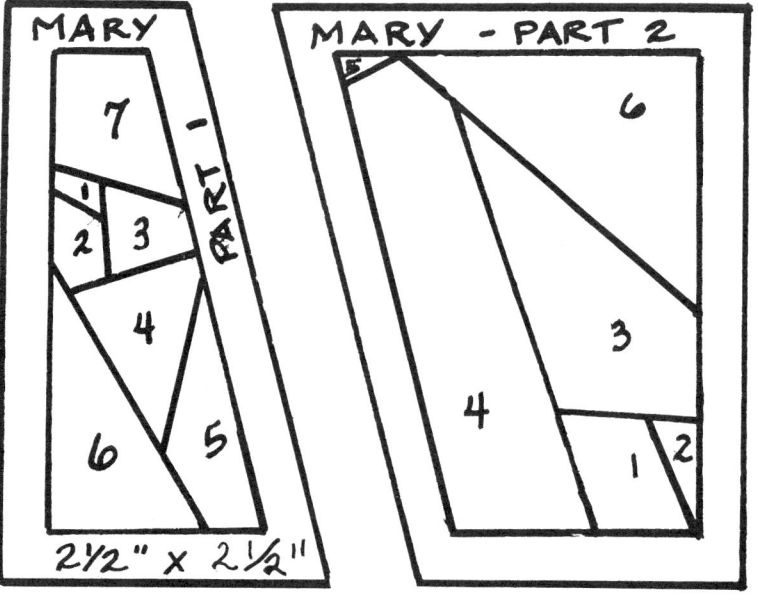

Mary is usually portrayed in shades of blue, but you can use the colors of your choice

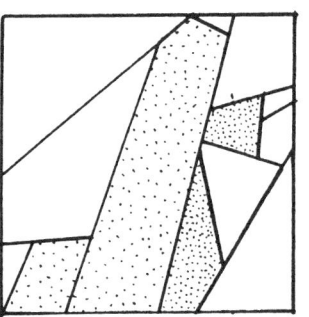

1

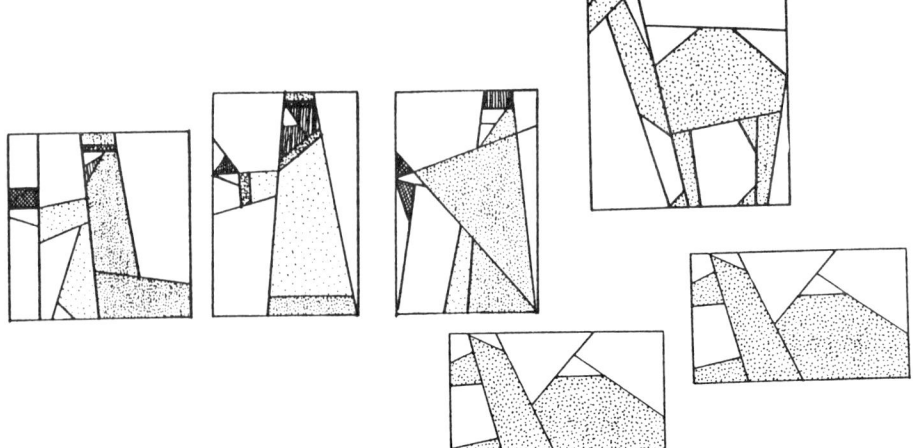

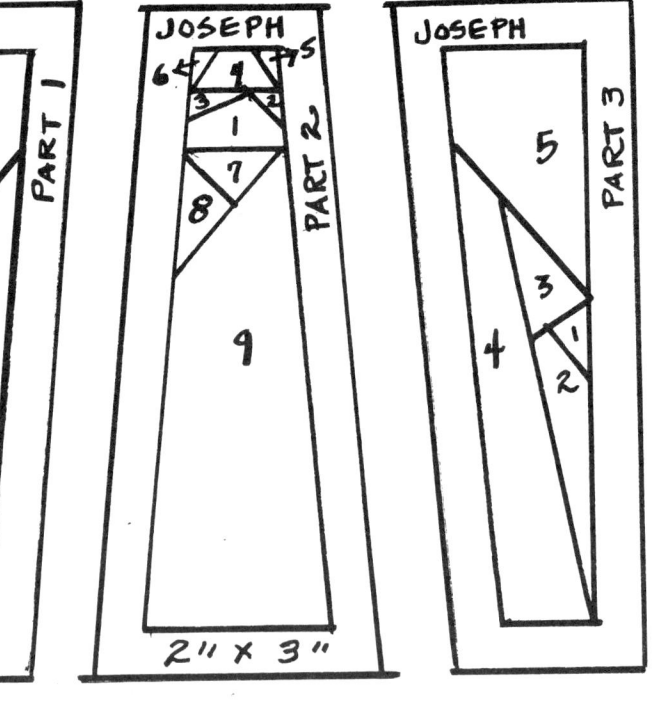

JOSEPH — PART 1

JOSEPH — PART 2

2" X 3"

JOSEPH — PART 3

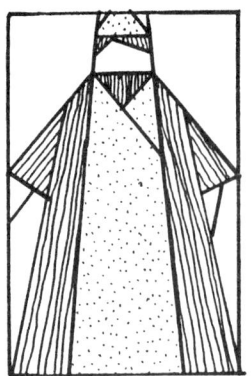

Joseph's robe is illustrated here in a tiny stripe. I feel that is an appropriate type of fabric for a man of his day. There are many small homespun fabrics available on the market from which to choose.

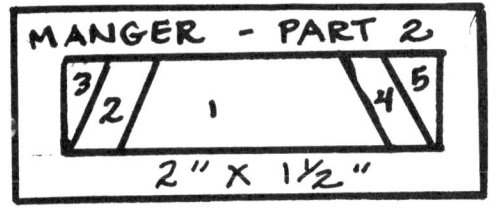

MANGER - PART 1

Piece one in the manger can be done with gold lame to present the feeling of a halo. If you do this, be sure to use an interfacing on the lame so it won't fray out.

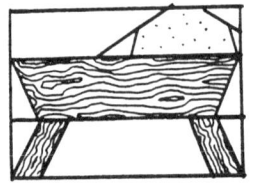

MANGER - PART 2

2" X 1½"

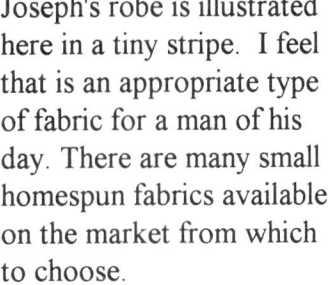

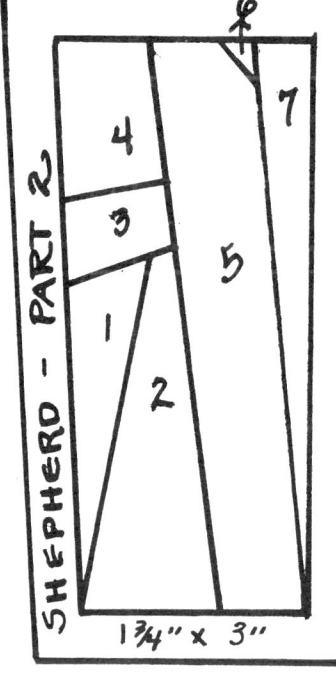

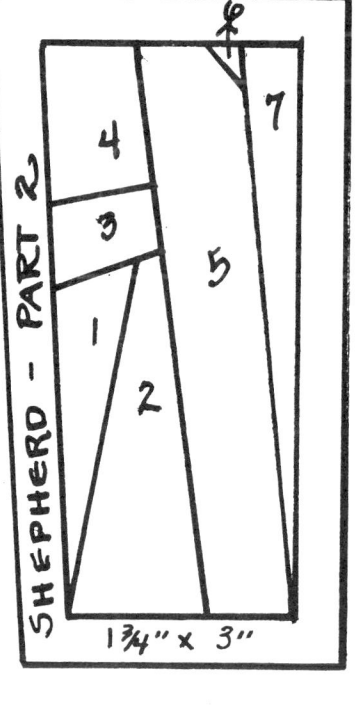

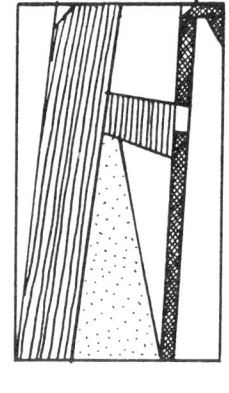

SHEPHERD - PART 1

5 6 7
1
2
4 3

SHEPHERD - PART 2

6
4
7
3
5
1
2

1¾" x 3"

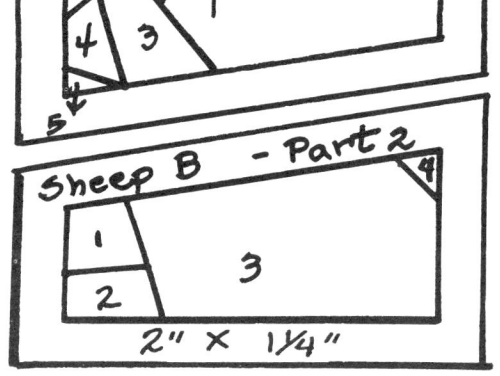

Sheep A - Part 2

6
5
7
1 2 3 4

2" x 1½"

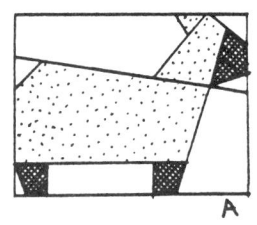

A

Search for the perfect fabric for the sheep for they are very important to the scene. You can include more sheep and more shepherds too if you like.

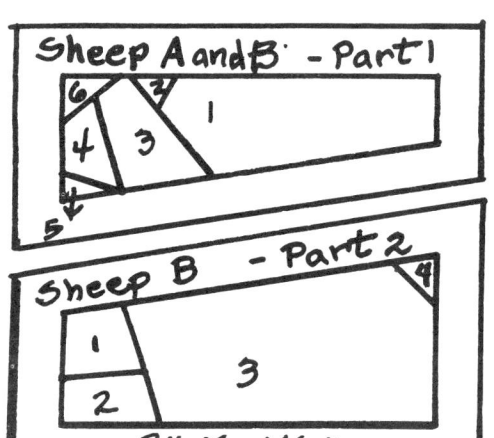

Sheep A and B - Part 1

6 3
4 3 1
5

Sheep B - Part 2

4
1
3
2

2" x 1¼"

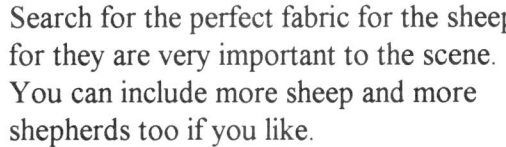

B

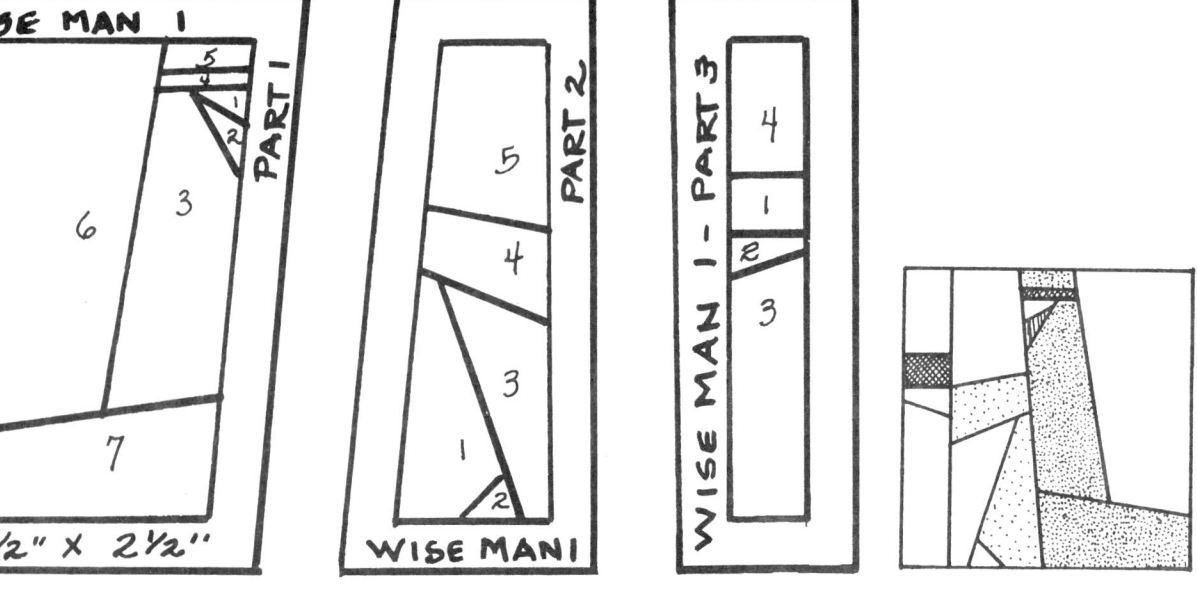

WISE MAN 1 — PART 1
2½" × 2½"

PART 2
WISE MAN 1

WISE MAN 1 — PART 3

The wise men should be made in rich elegant fabrics. Their gifts can be made with lame or other shiny fabrics.

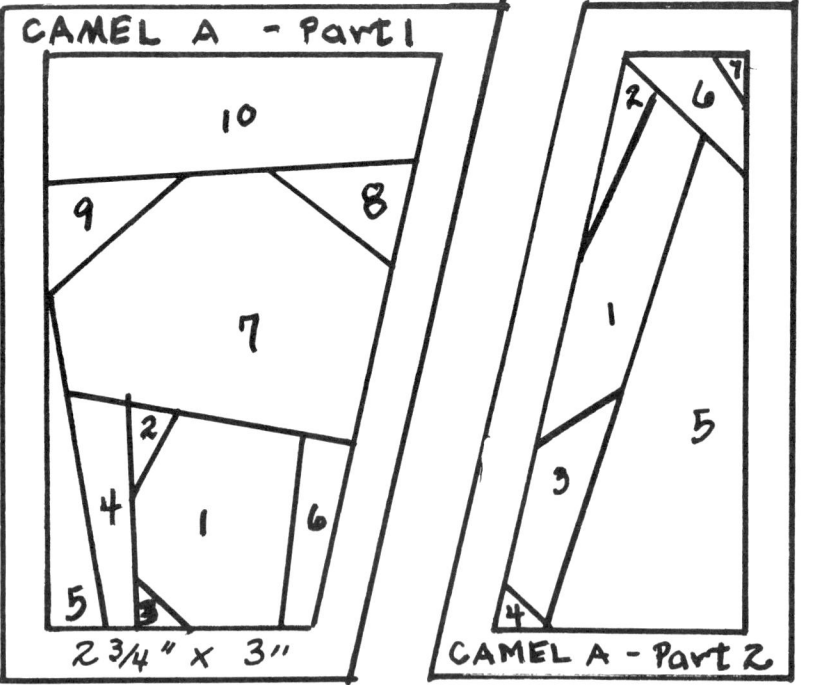

CAMEL A — Part 1
2 ¾" × 3"

CAMEL A — Part 2

If you want to put rich furnishings on the camels, be sure to layer them on with the base fabric of the main body piece as you put the patterns together.

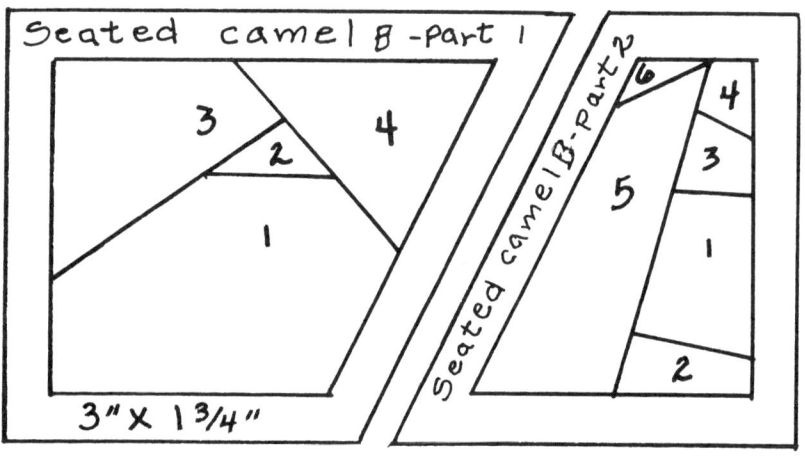

Seated camel B — Part 1
3" × 1 ¾"

Seated camel B — Part 2

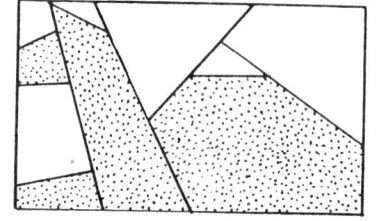

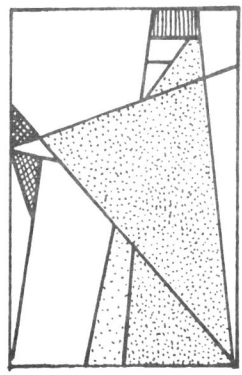

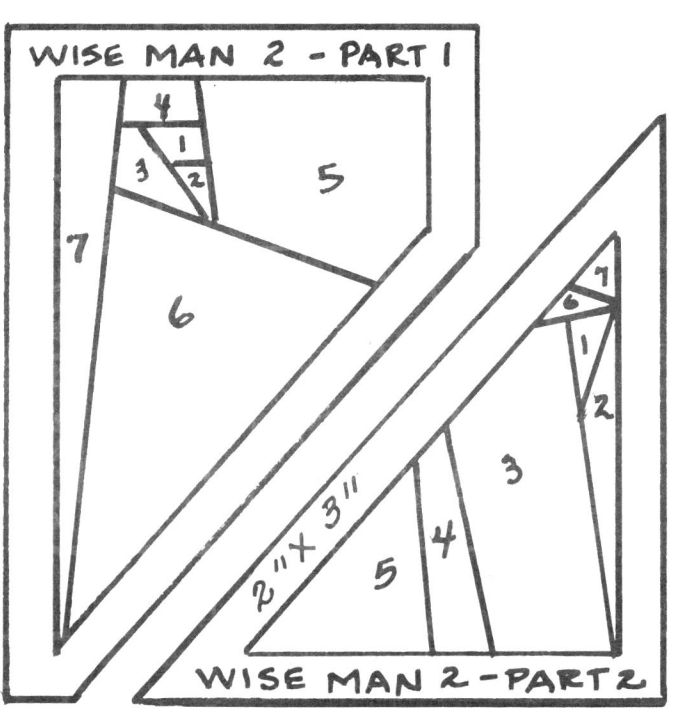

WISE MAN 2 - PART 1

4
1
3
2
5
7
6

2" X 3"

7
6
1
2
3
4
5

WISE MAN 2 - PART 2

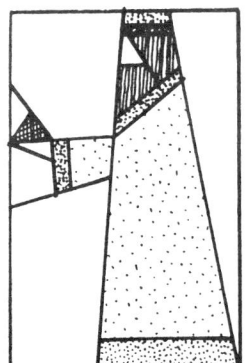

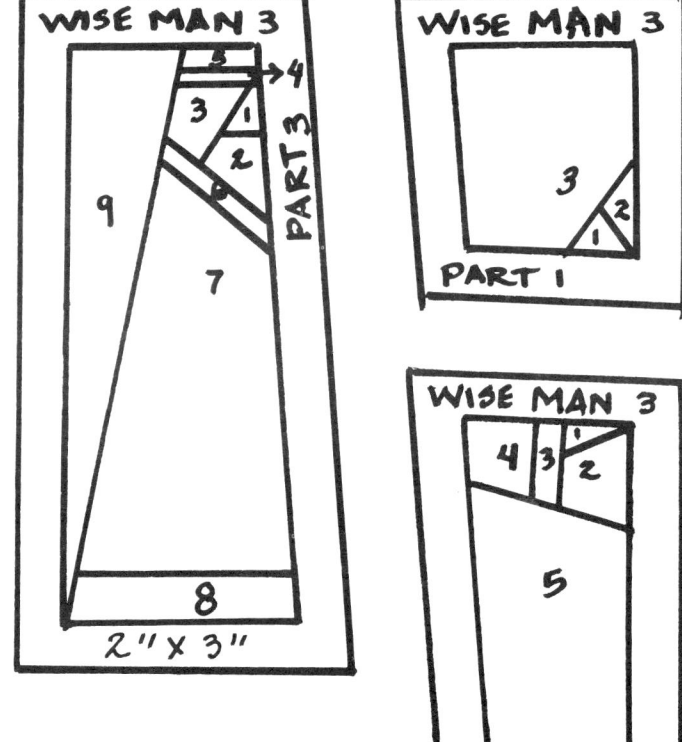

WISE MAN 3

5
4
3
1
2
6
9
7
8

2" X 3"

PART 3

WISE MAN 3

3
1
2

PART 1

WISE MAN 3

4 3 1
2
5

PART 2

Piece part one and part two
and remove the paper backing.
Now you can sew them to-
gether and add part three
after you get it pieced.

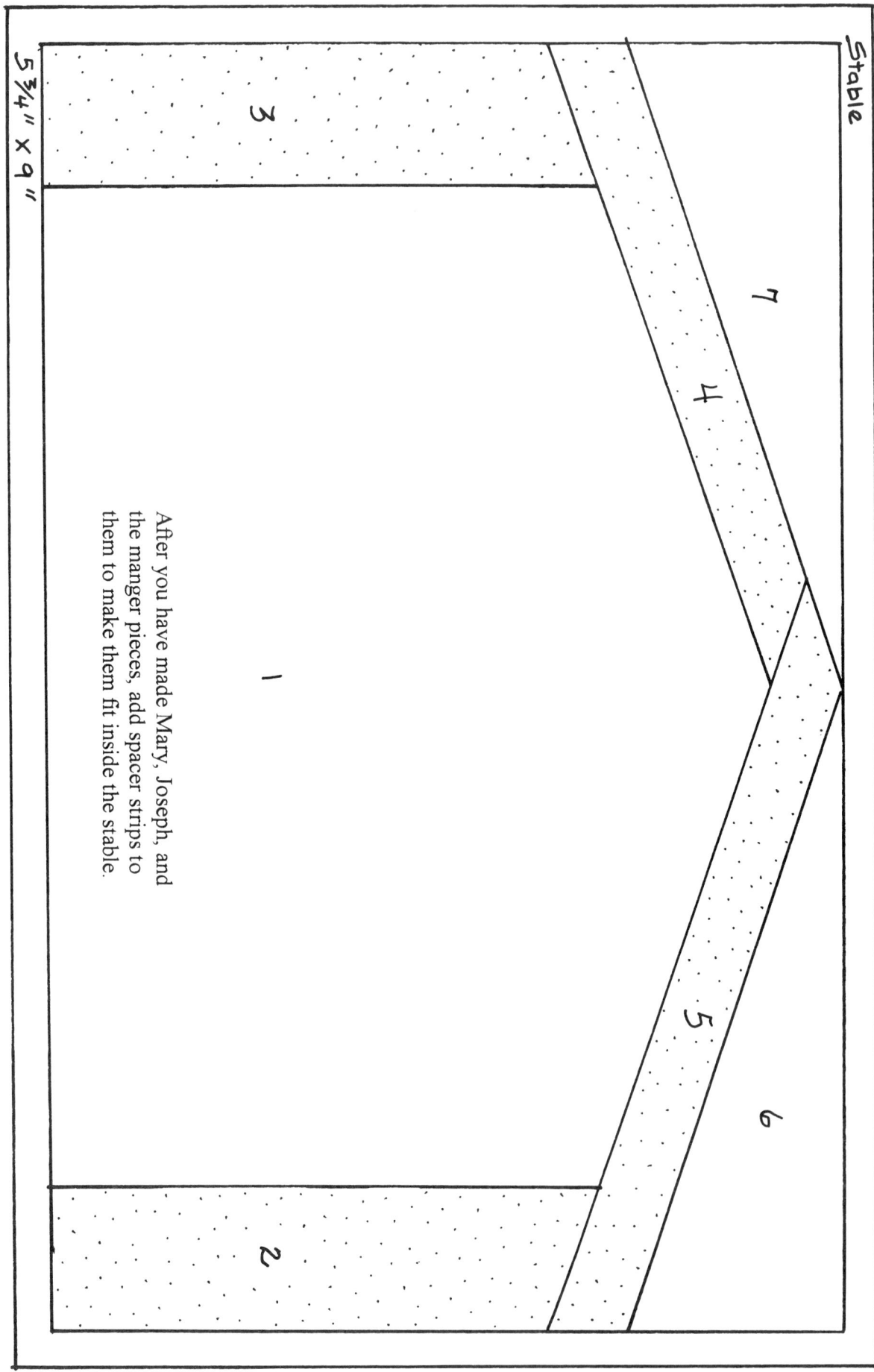

Stable

5 3/4" x 9"

7

4

3

1

6

5

2

After you have made Mary, Joseph, and the manger pieces, add spacer strips to them to make them fit inside the stable.

SNOWMEN

Three little snowmen will help to make the season jolly. All need bead or sequin eyes. Two need bead buttons and mouths. While each take several parts to complete, they are quick and easy if you take them one part at a time.

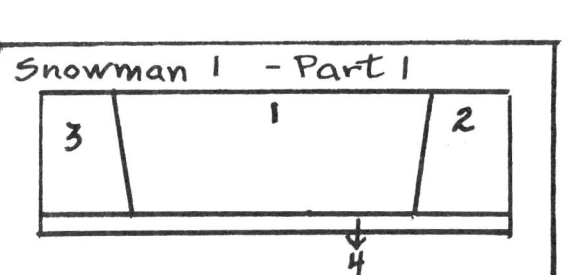

Snowman 1 - Part 1

3 | 1 | 2
4

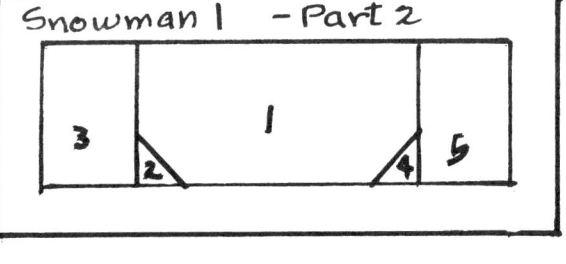

Snowman 1 - Part 2

3 | 1 | 2 4 5

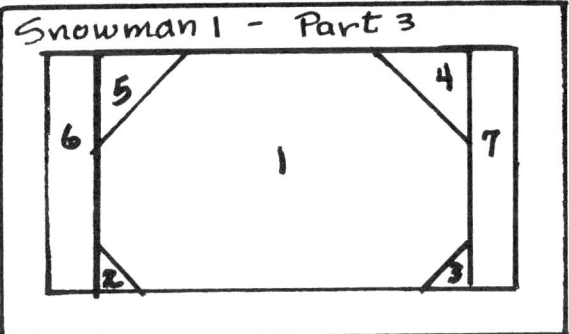

Snowman 1 - Part 3

5 4
6 1 7
2 3

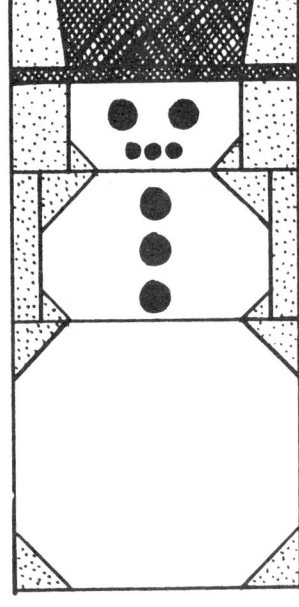

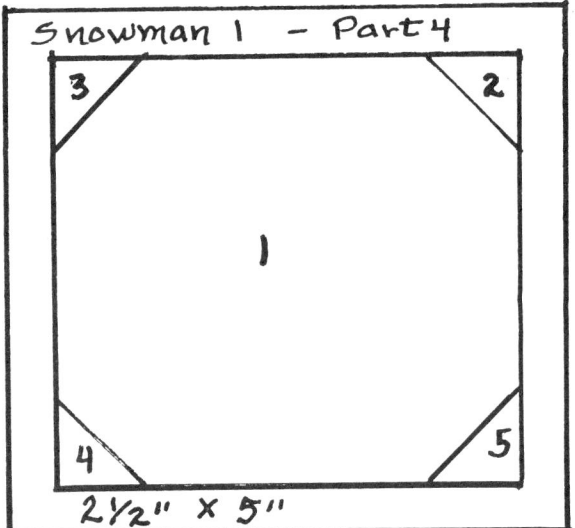

Snowman 1 - Part 4

3 2
1
4 5

2½" X 5"

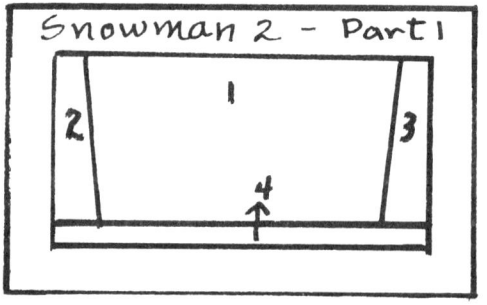

Snowman 2 - Part 1

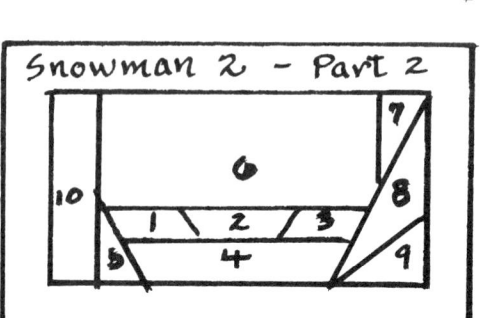

Snowman 2 – Part 2

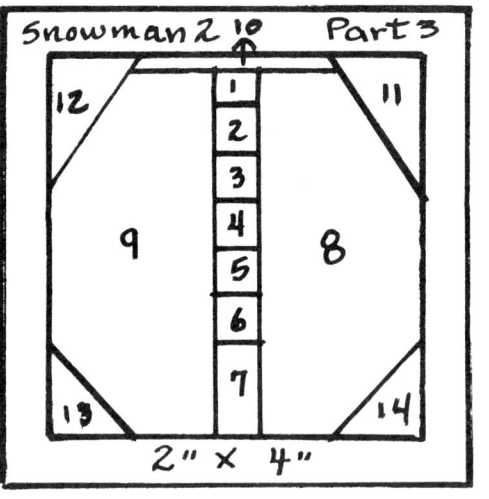

Snowman 2 ¹⁰ Part 3

2" × 4"

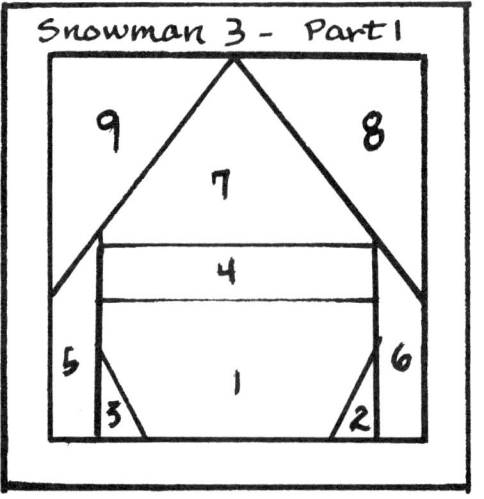

Snowman 3 - Part 1

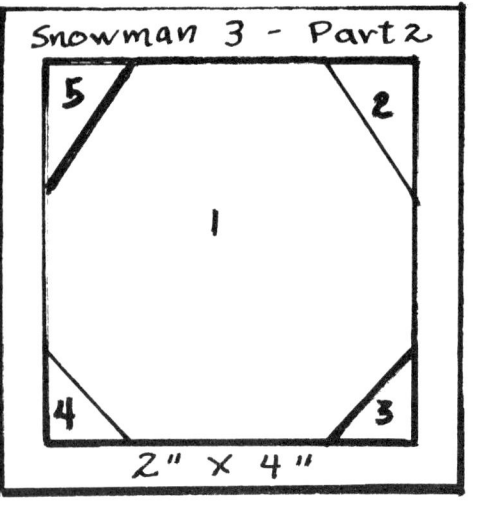

Snowman 3 - Part 2

2" × 4"

STAR

Five point stars are fun to use and make with this easy pattern. I have put them here in two sizes but you can enlarge or shrink them to fit your personal needs.

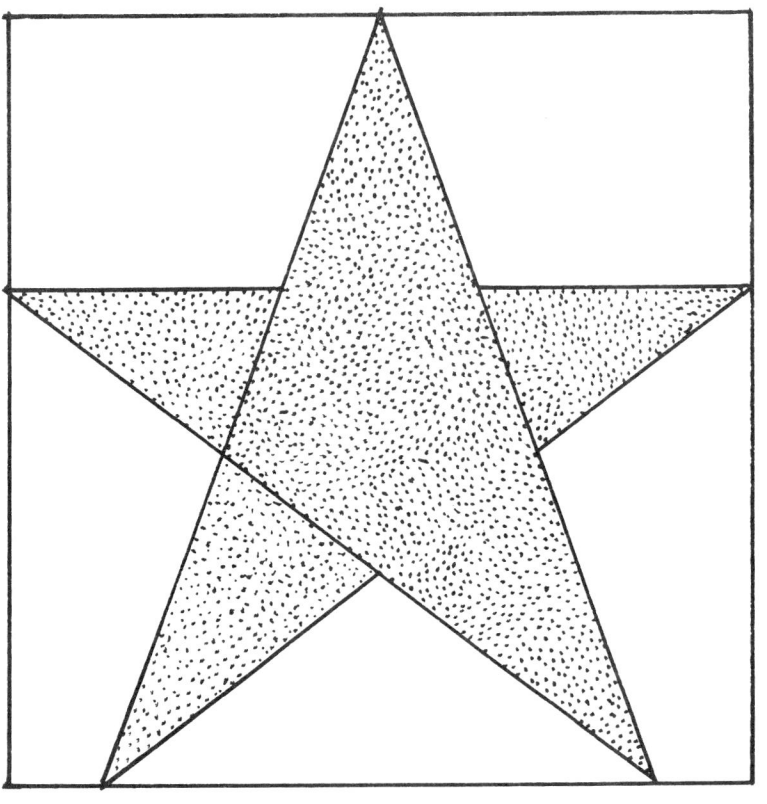

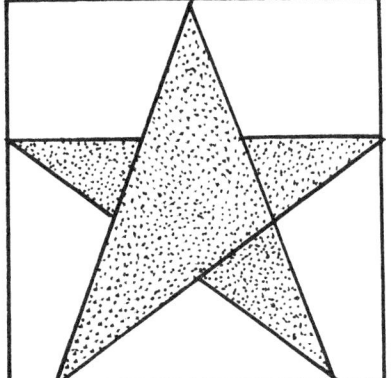

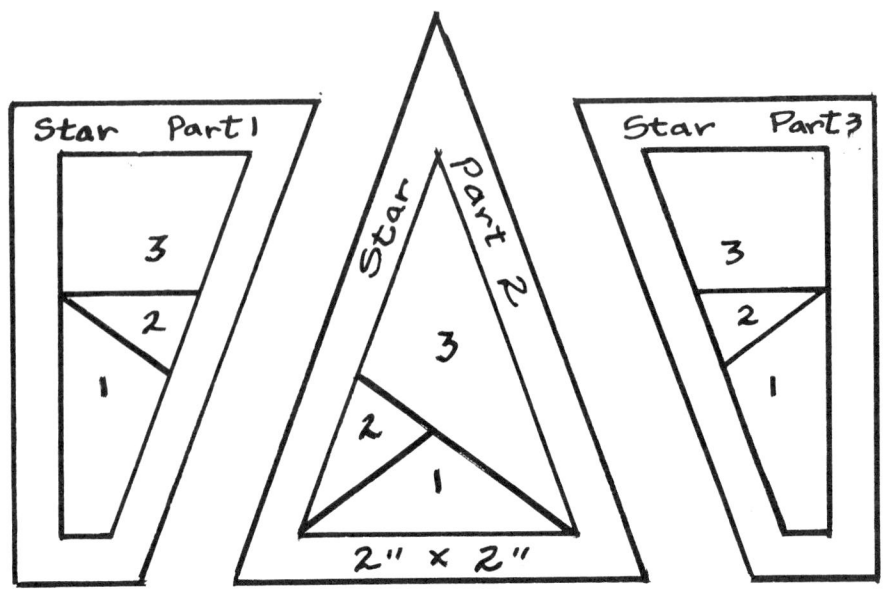

Star Part 1

3
2
1

Star Part 2

3
2
1

2" × 2"

Star Part 3

3
2
1

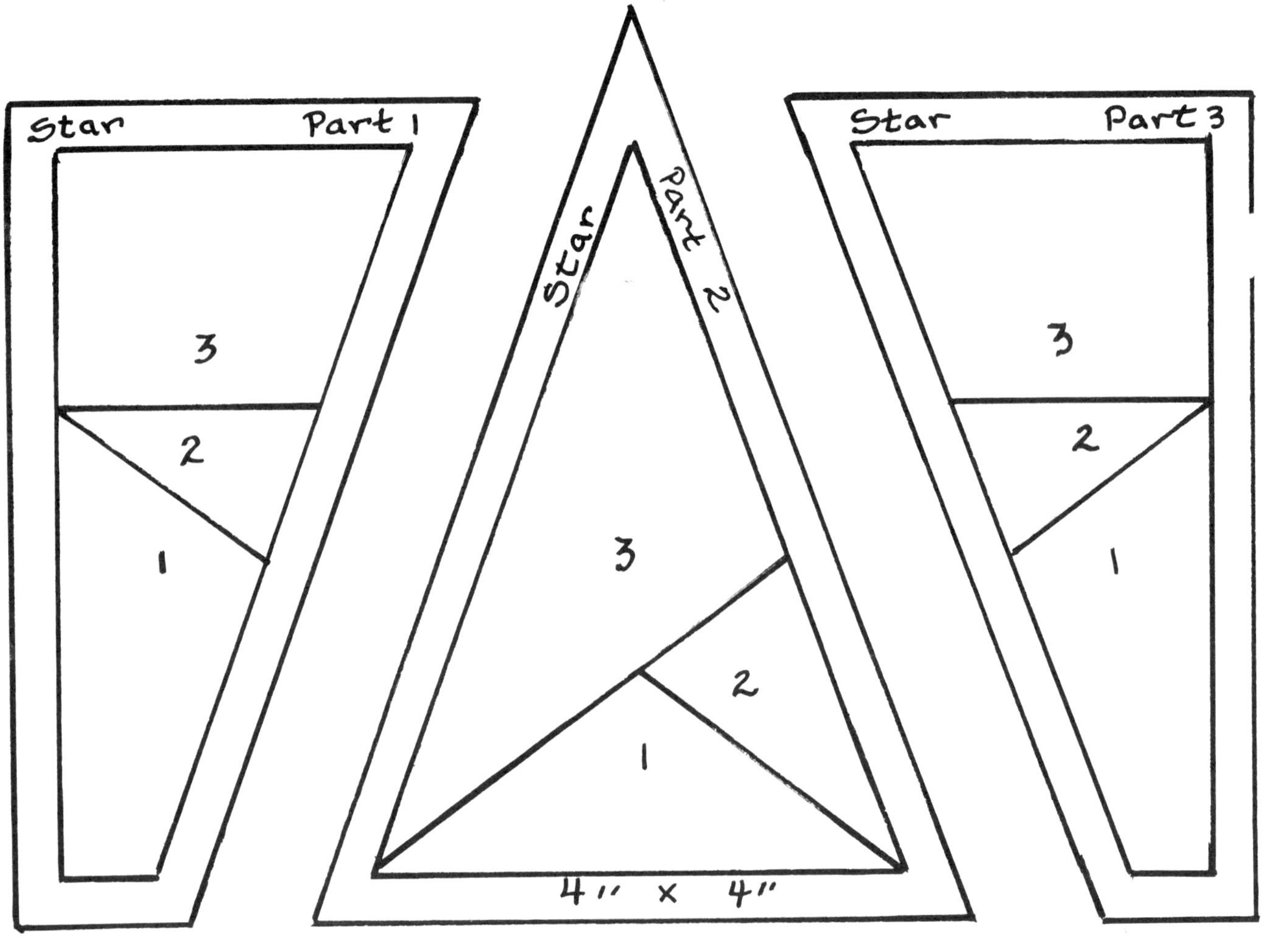

Star Part 1

3
2
1

Star Part 2

3
2
1

4" × 4"

Star Part 3

3
2
1

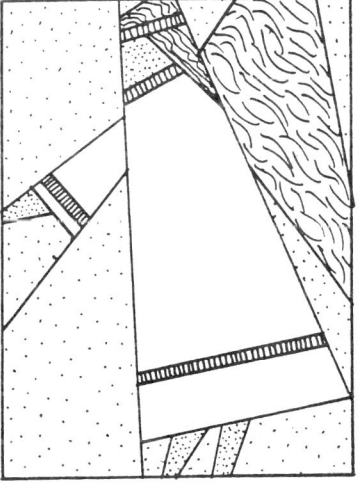

ANGELS

Angels are very popular right now so I have included designs for three different styles. Finding the right fabrics will be fun. The designs all include little stripes of trim at the neck and sleeve or hem. This can be made with shiny fabrics or even lame. If you use fabrics that ravel easily, be sure to interface them.

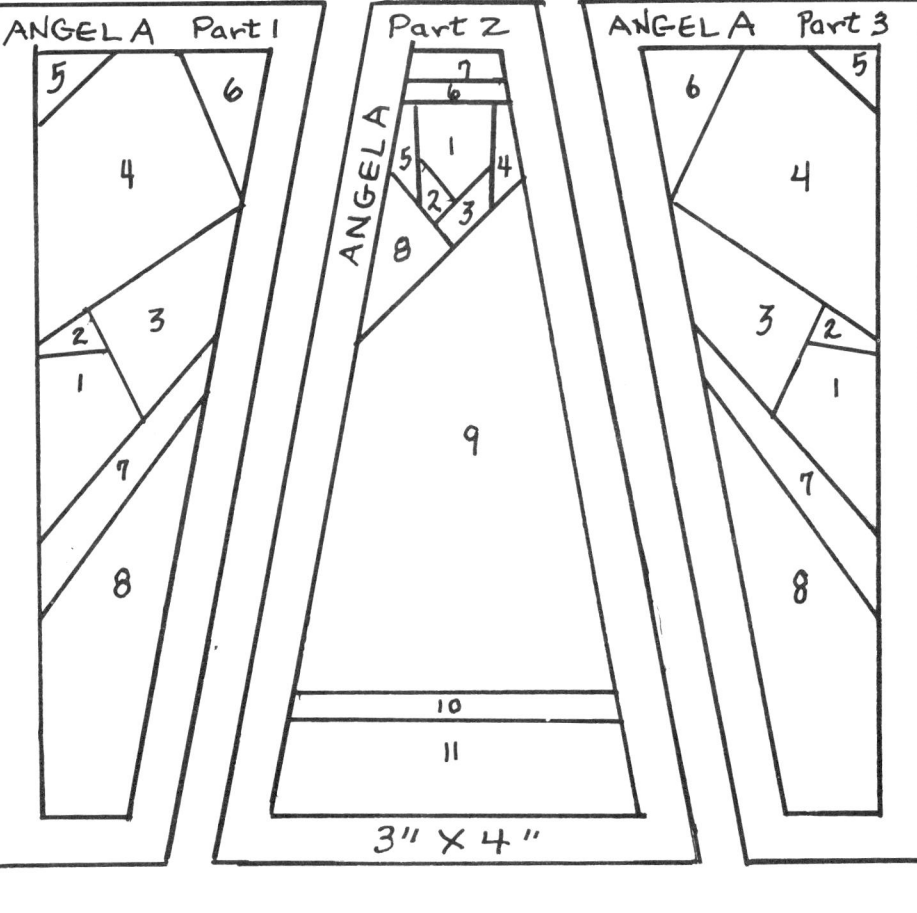

ANGEL B
Part 1
ANGEL B
Part 2
3" x 4"
ANGEL B
Part 3

ANGEL C Part 1
Part 2
ANGEL C
ANGEL C
Part 3
3" x 4"

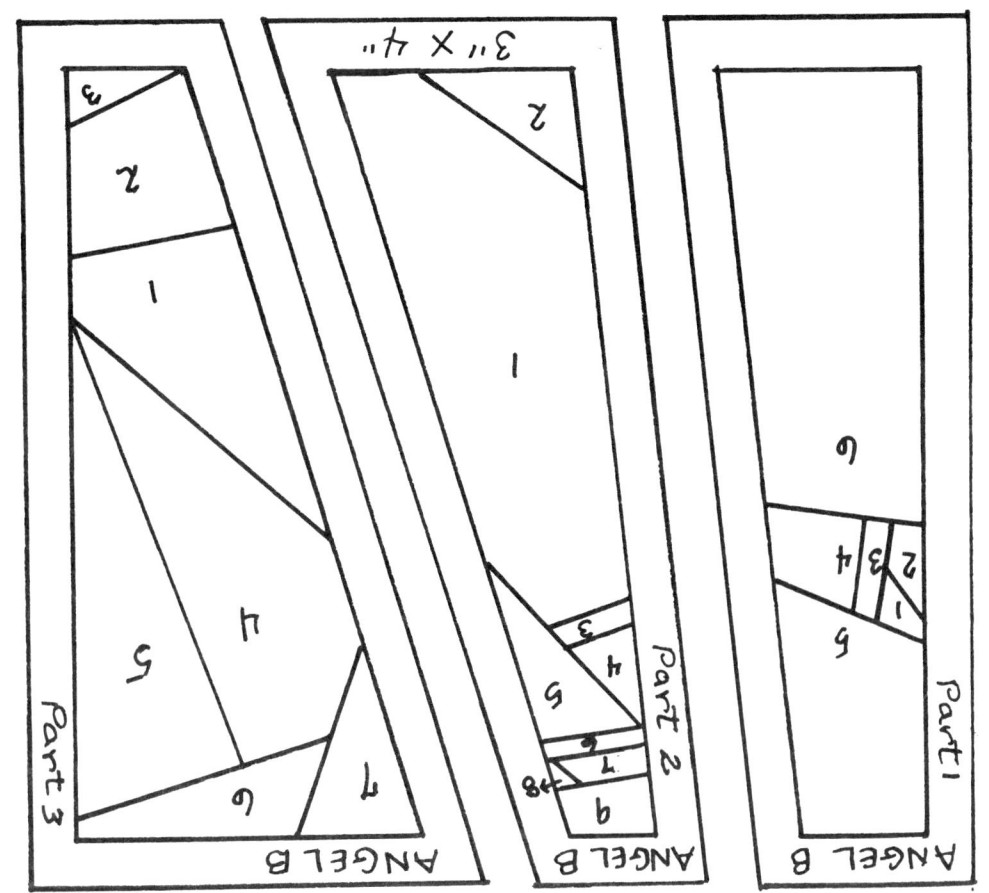

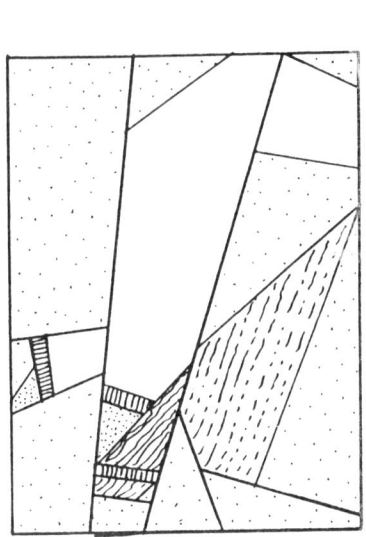

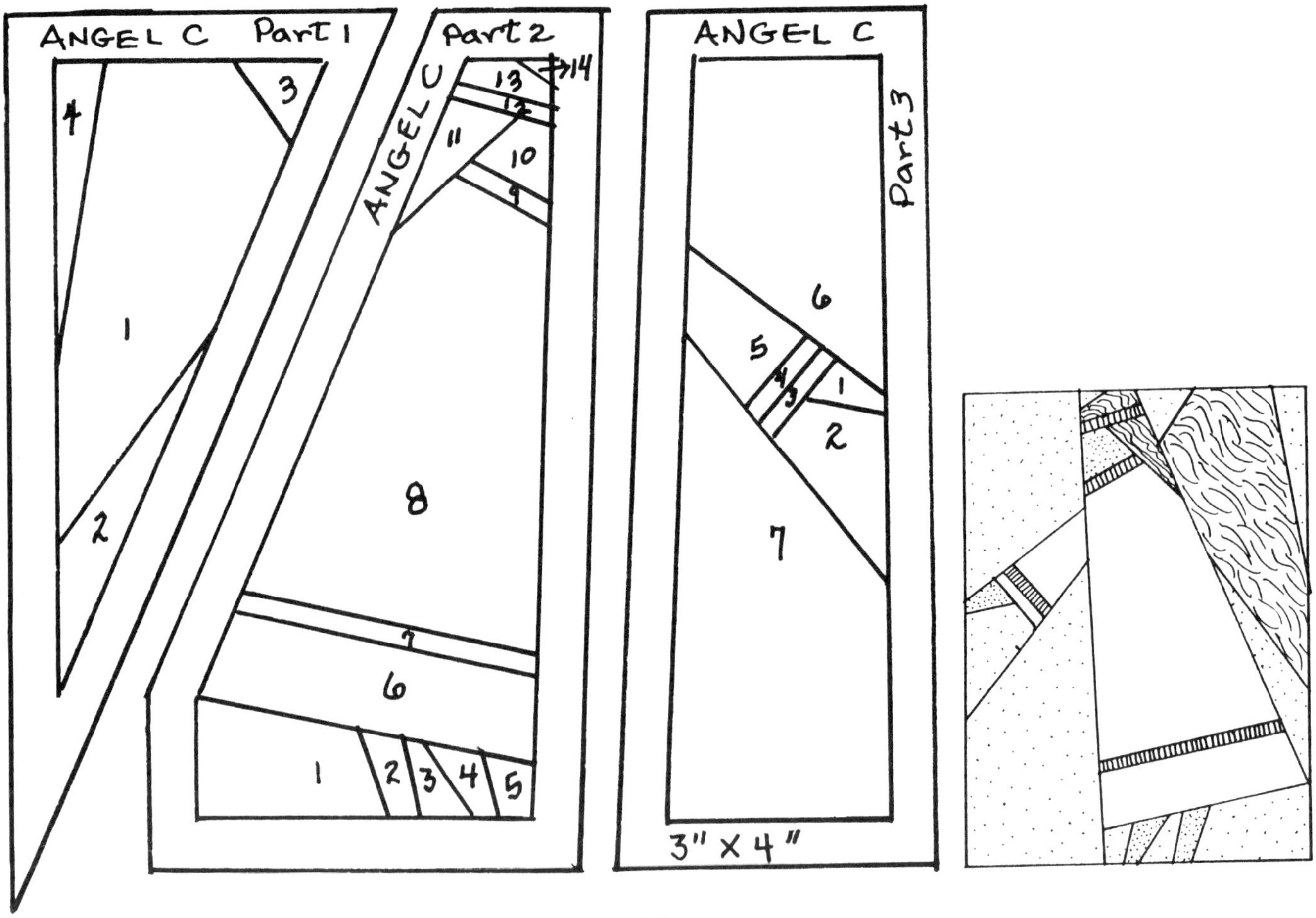

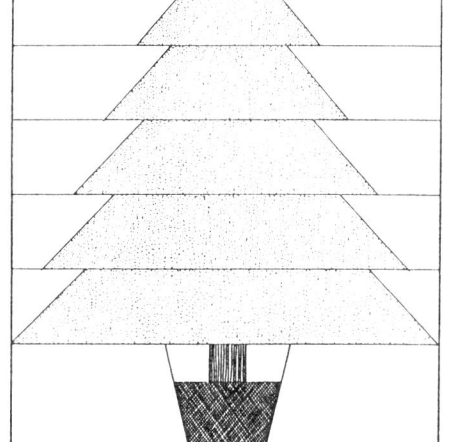

CHRISTMAS TREE

 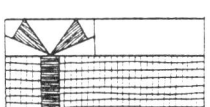  

Here is an easy Christmas tree pattern which can be made with a different fabric for each row, or one overall fabric. It is large enough to decorate with beads or embellish with shiny cords, ribbons or tinsel. Then make a group of presents to place around the tree. The presents are small but effective and are easy to construct. To assemble these components into a scene, add spacer strips between the presents and top them with a strip to bring them to the height of the tree.

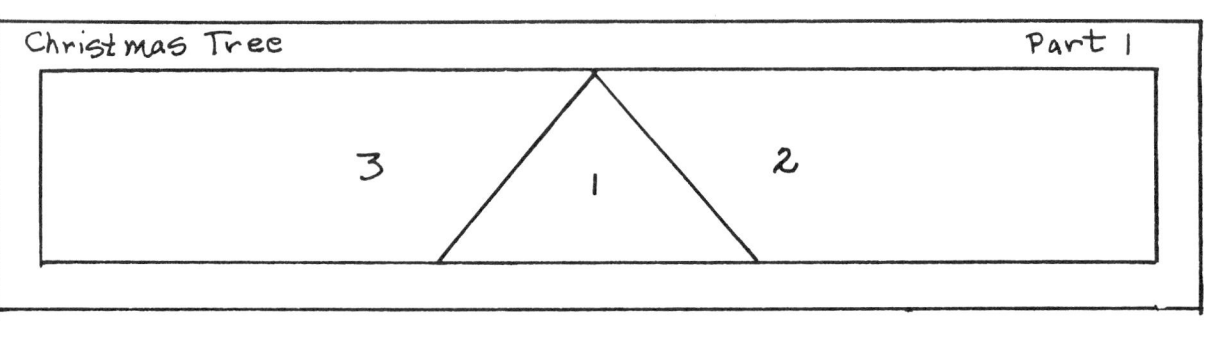

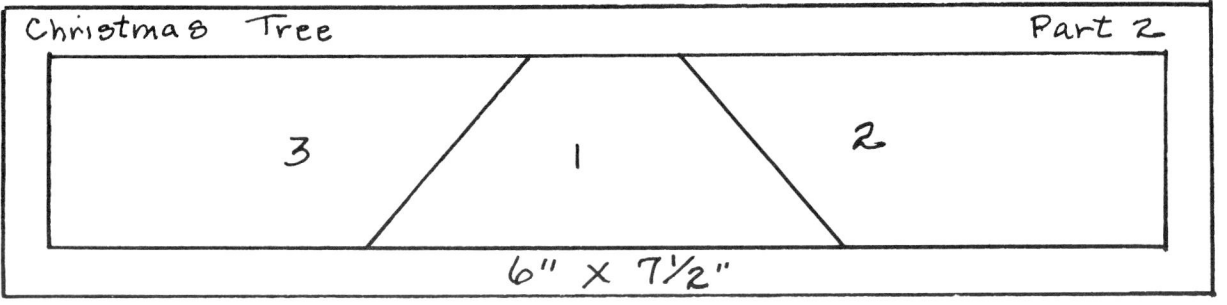

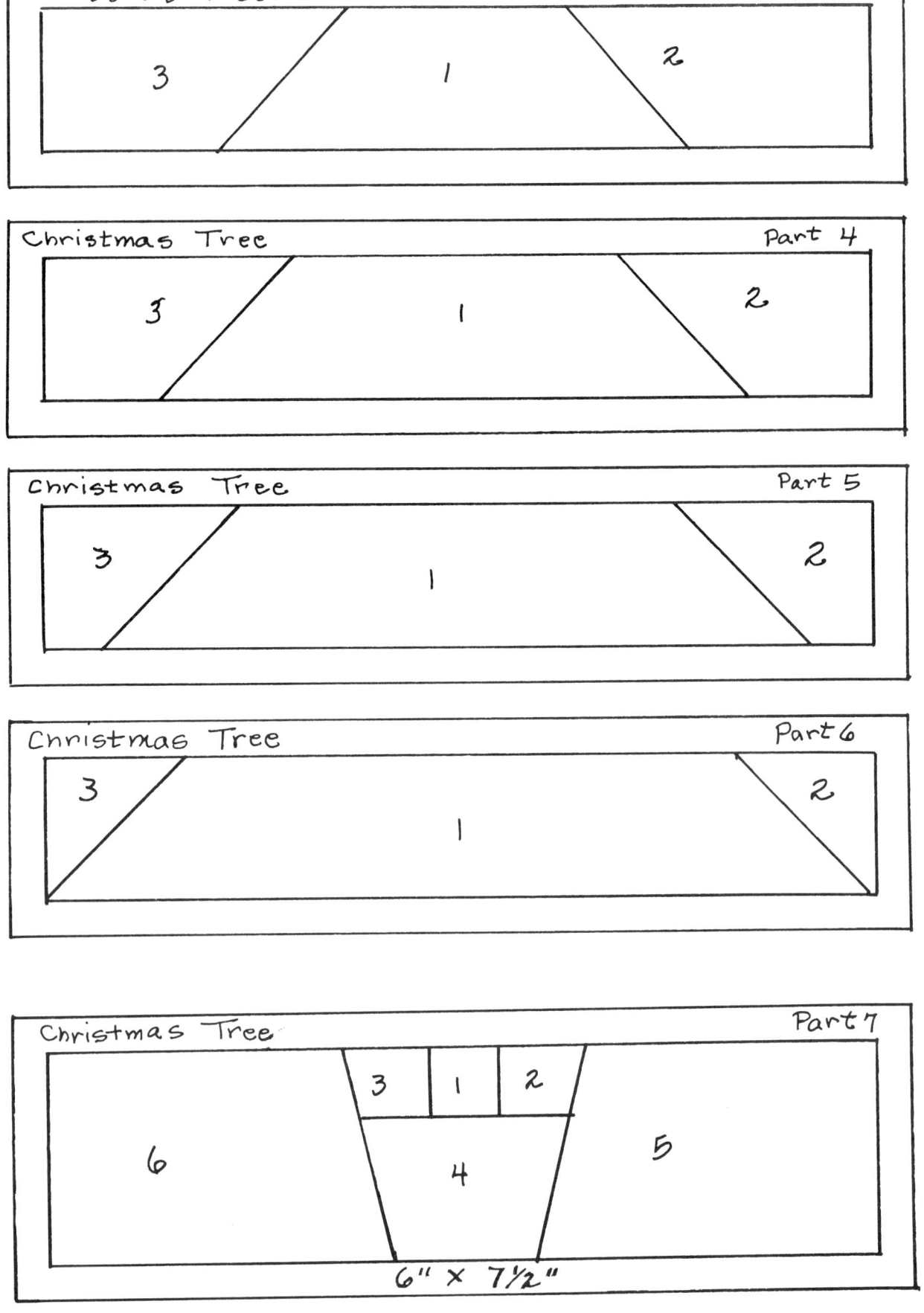

Christmas Tree   Part 3

3   1   2

Christmas Tree   Part 4

3   1   2

Christmas Tree   Part 5

3   1   2

Christmas Tree   Part 6

3   1   2

Christmas Tree   Part 7

6   3   1   2   5

4

6" × 7½"

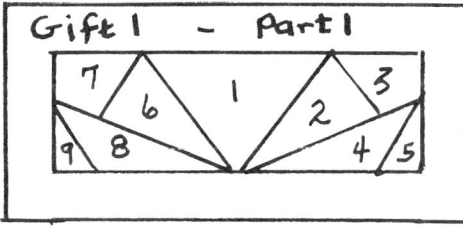

Gift 1 - Part 1

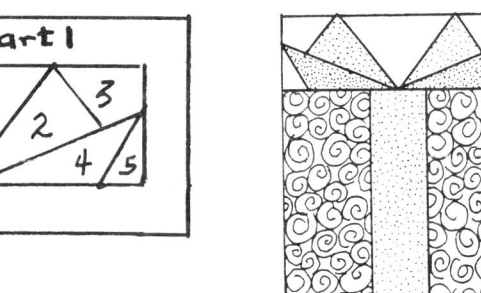

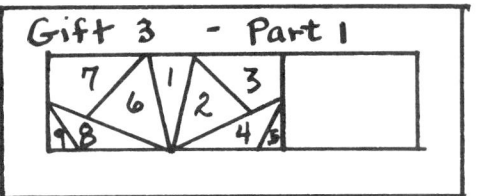

Gift 1 - Part 2

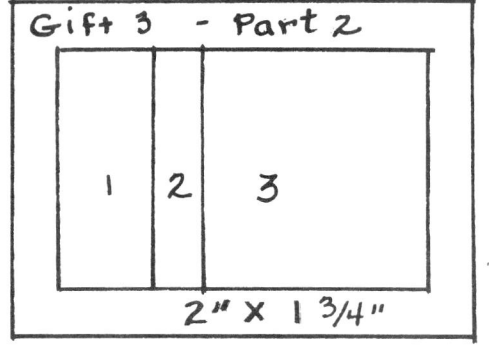

2" X 2 ½"

PRESENTS

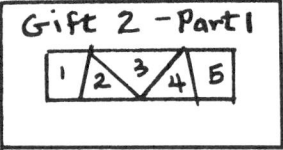

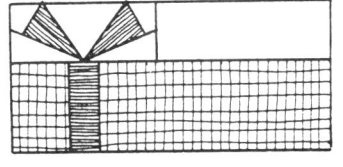

Gift 2 - Part 1

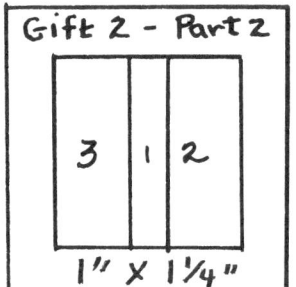

Gift 2 - Part 2

1" X 1 ¼"

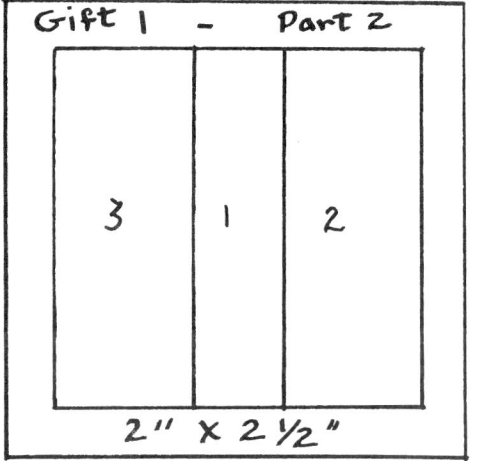

Gift 3 - Part 1

Gift 3 - Part 2

2" X 1 ¾"

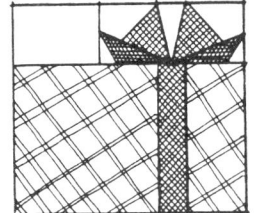

Gift 4 - Part 1

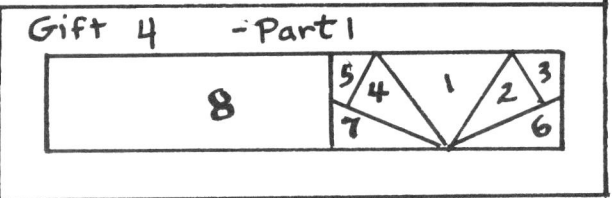

Gift 4 - Part 2

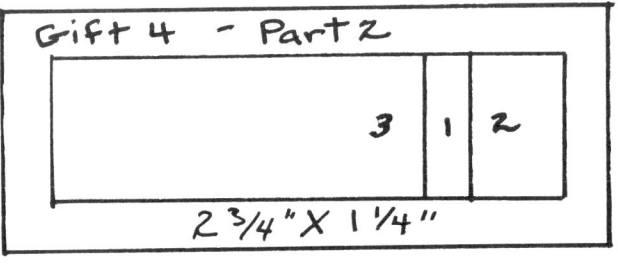

2 ¾" X 1 ¼"

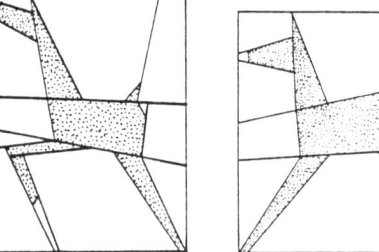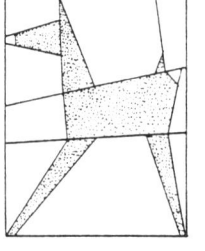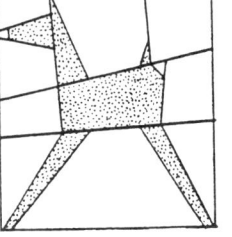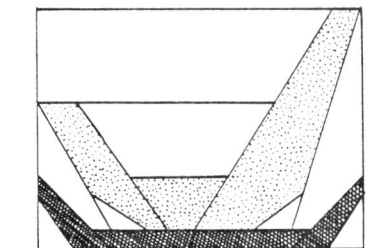

SLEIGH AND REINDEER

I have designed three different little deer to pull the sleigh. This can be enlarged to create a wall hanging of the sleigh, reindeer and one of the Santas. Have fun with the dear little deer. To make a scene like you see above, sew spacers strips between the pieced blocks.

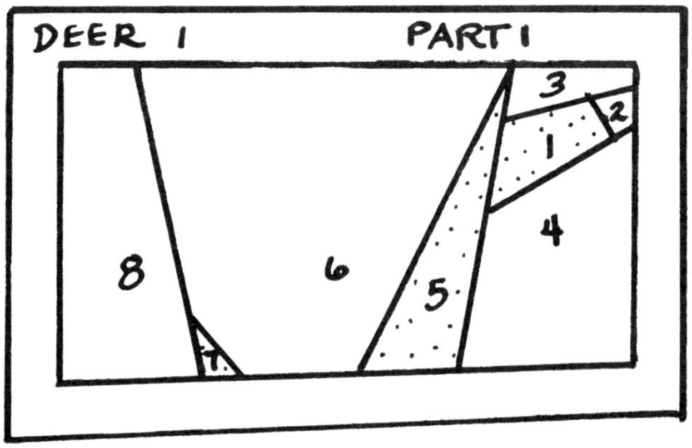

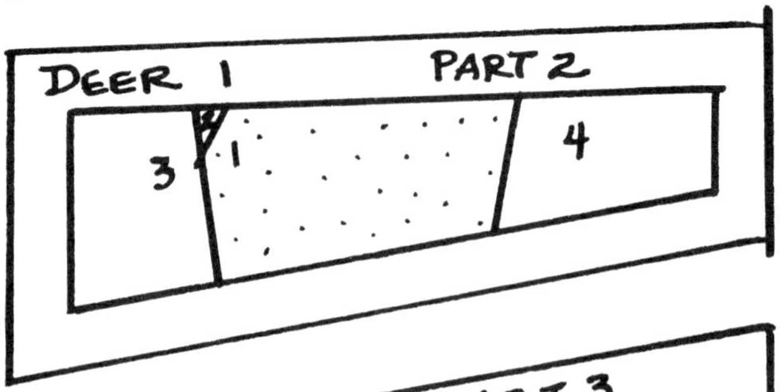

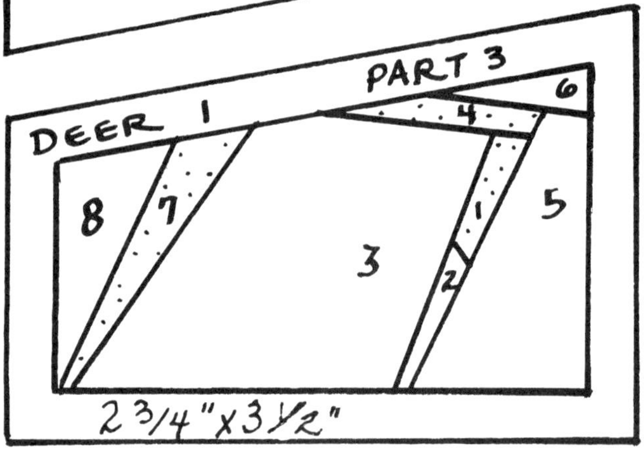

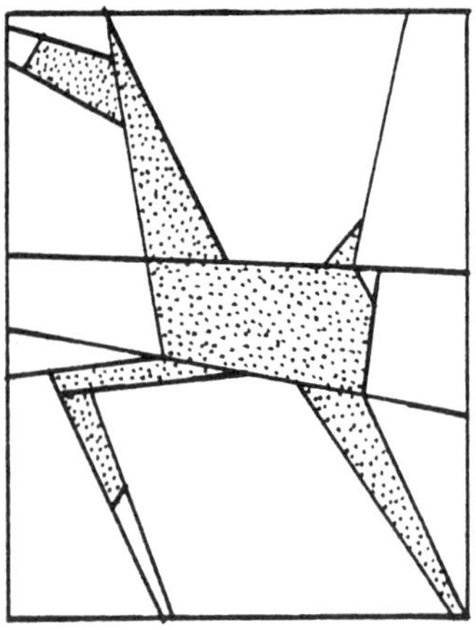

DEER 1   PART 1

3
2
1
4
5
6
8
7

DEER 1   PART 2

3 1   4

PART 3
DEER 1   6
4
8 7   5
1
3
2
2 3/4" x 3 1/2"

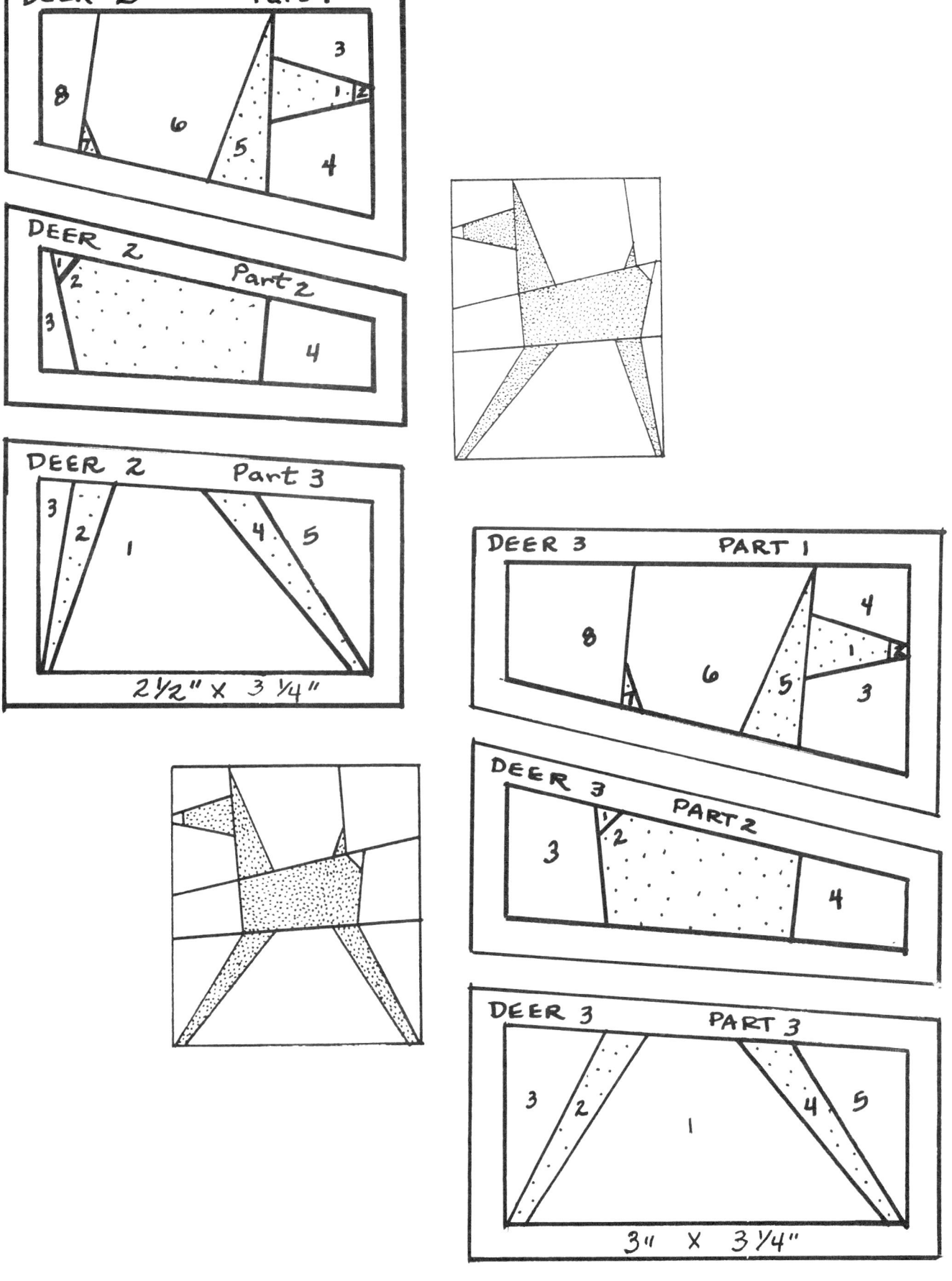

DEER 2 Part 1

3
8
1 2
6
5
4

DEER 2 Part 2

1
2
3
4

DEER 2 Part 3

3
2
1
4 5

2½" X 3¼"

DEER 3 PART 1

4
8
1 2
6
5 3

DEER 3 PART 2

3
1
2
4

DEER 3 PART 3

3
2
1
4 5

3" X 3¼"

17

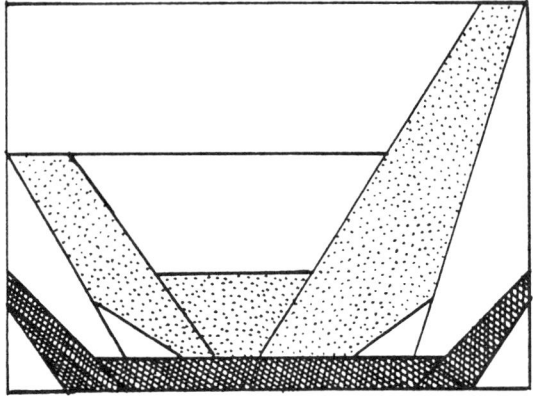

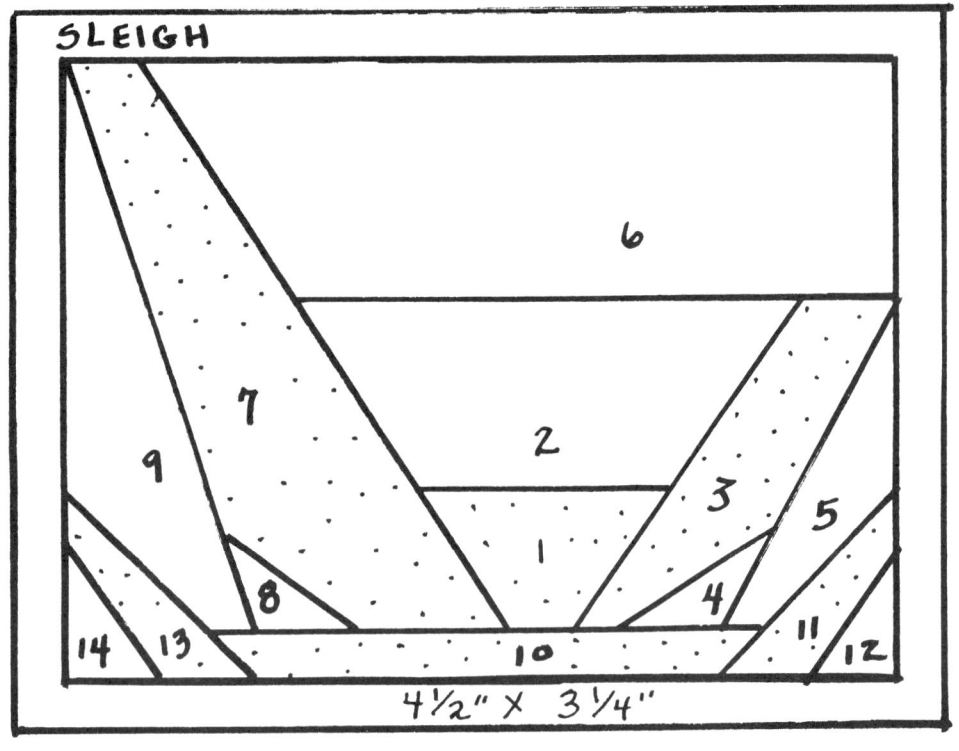

SLEIGH

6

7

2

9

3

1

5

8

4

14 13

10

11

12

4½" X 3¼"

18

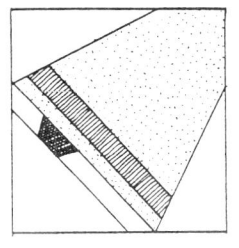
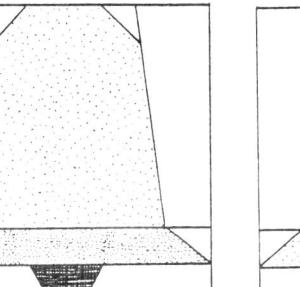
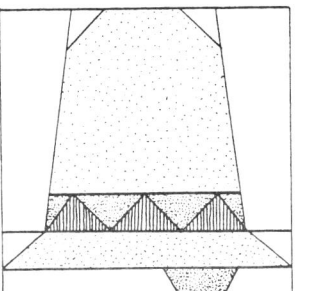
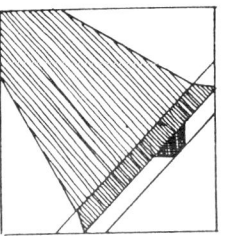

BELLS

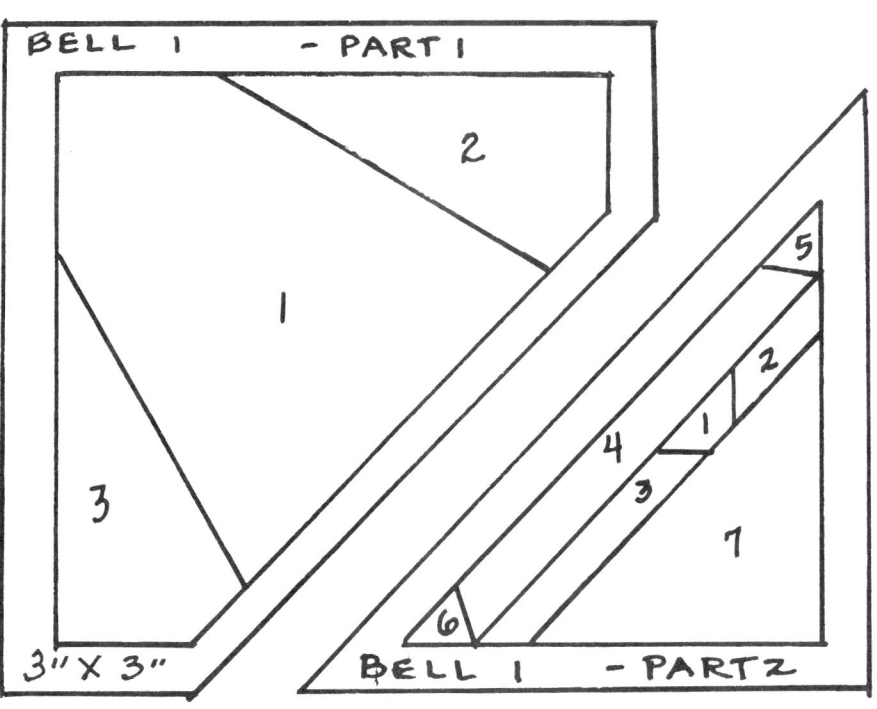

BELL 1 — PART 1

2

1

3

3" X 3"

BELL 1 — PART 2

5

2

4

1

3

7

6

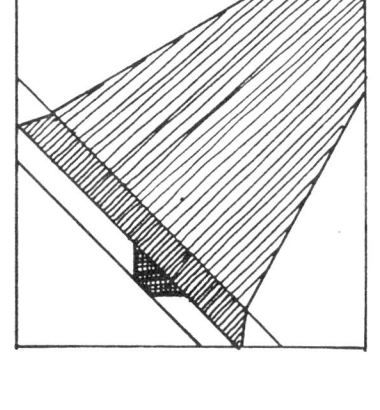

There are two types of bells here. Some are on the straight and the others are on point. They can be used together or separately. I think they would make a great border for a project.

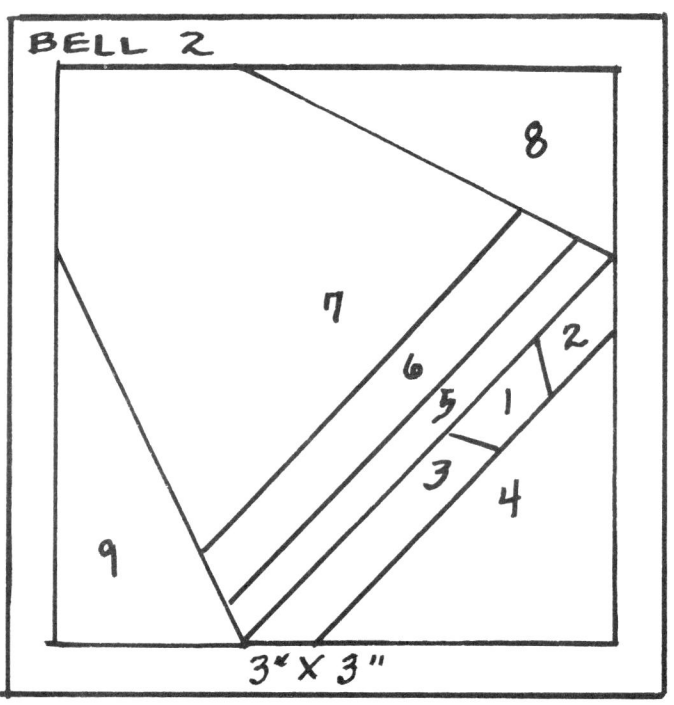

BELL 2

8

7

6

5

1

2

3

4

9

3" X 3"

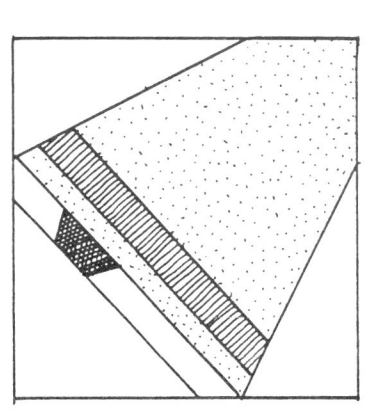

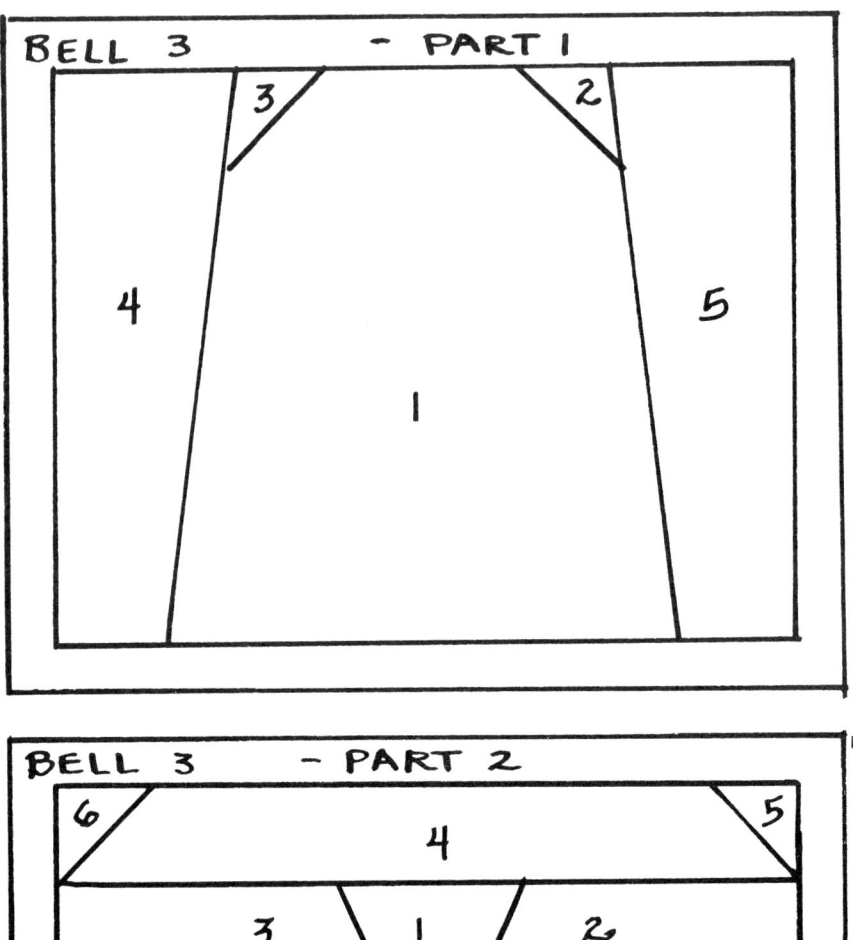

BELL 3   - PART I

3   2

4   1   5

BELL 3   - PART 2

6   4   5

3   1   2

4" X 4"

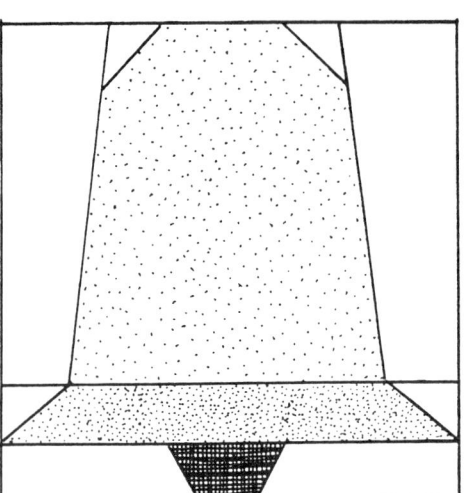

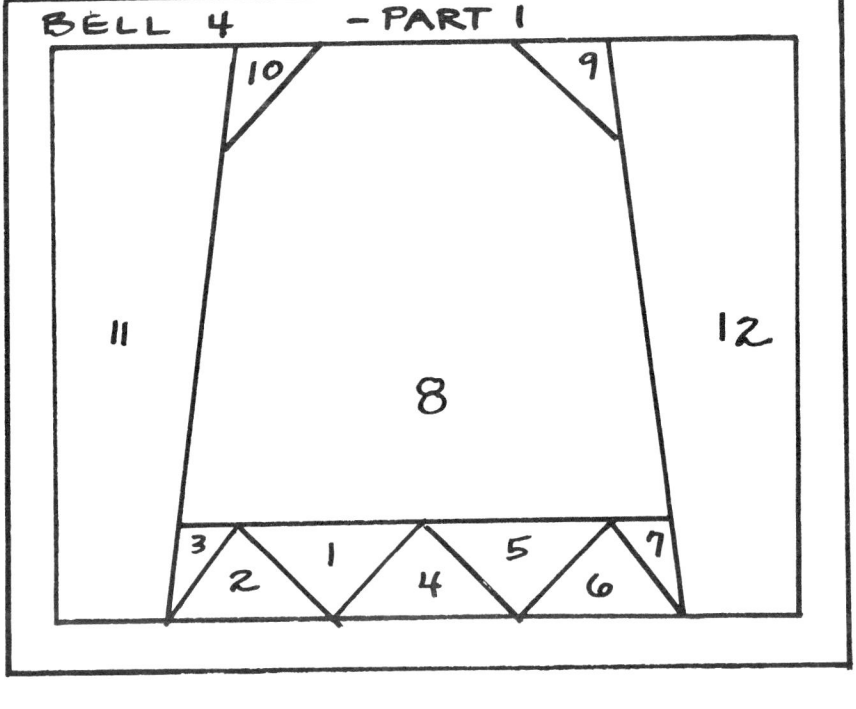

BELL 4 — PART 1

10   9

11   12

8

3   1   5   7
2   4   6

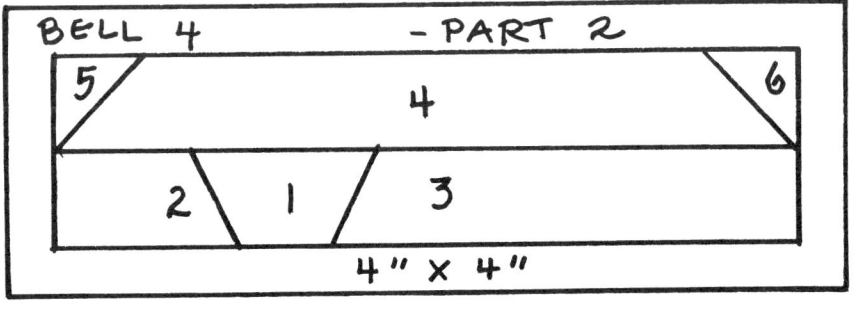

BELL 4 — PART 2

5   4   6

2   1   3

4" X 4"

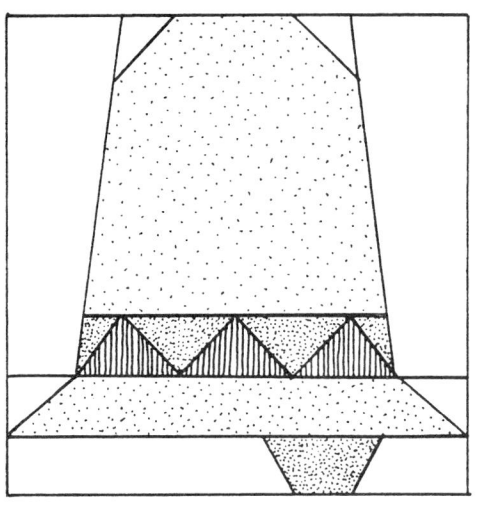

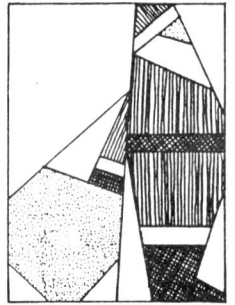  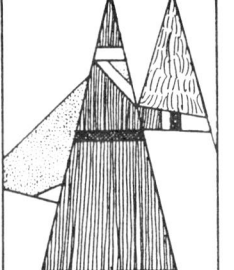

SANTA

Here is a series of Santas to try. Each has his own charm so choose the one that appeals to you and have a great time constructing him.

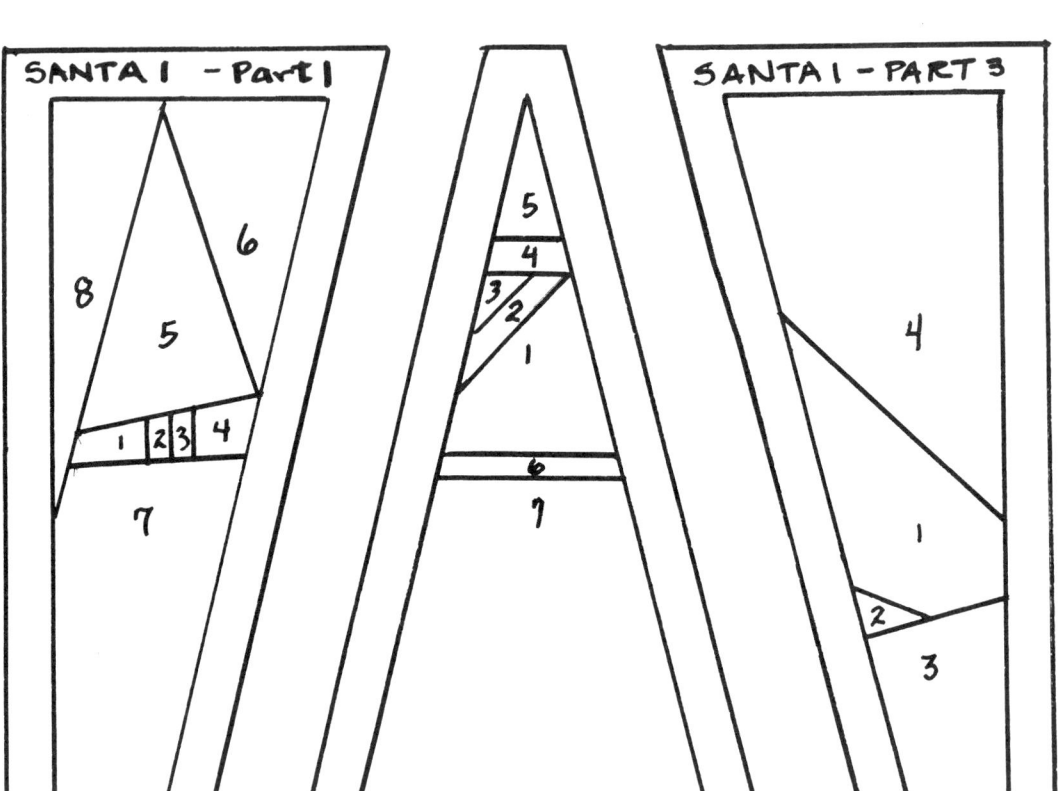

SANTA 1 - Part 1

8 6
5
1 2 3 4
7

4" x 4"

5
4
3 2
1
6
7

SANTA 1 - PART 2

SANTA 1 - PART 3

4
1
2
3

This old fashioned Santa carries a tree as well as the bag full of toys on his back.

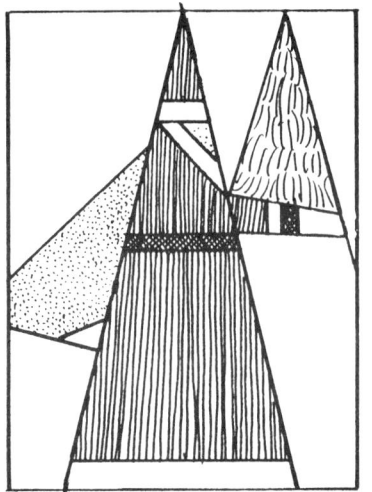

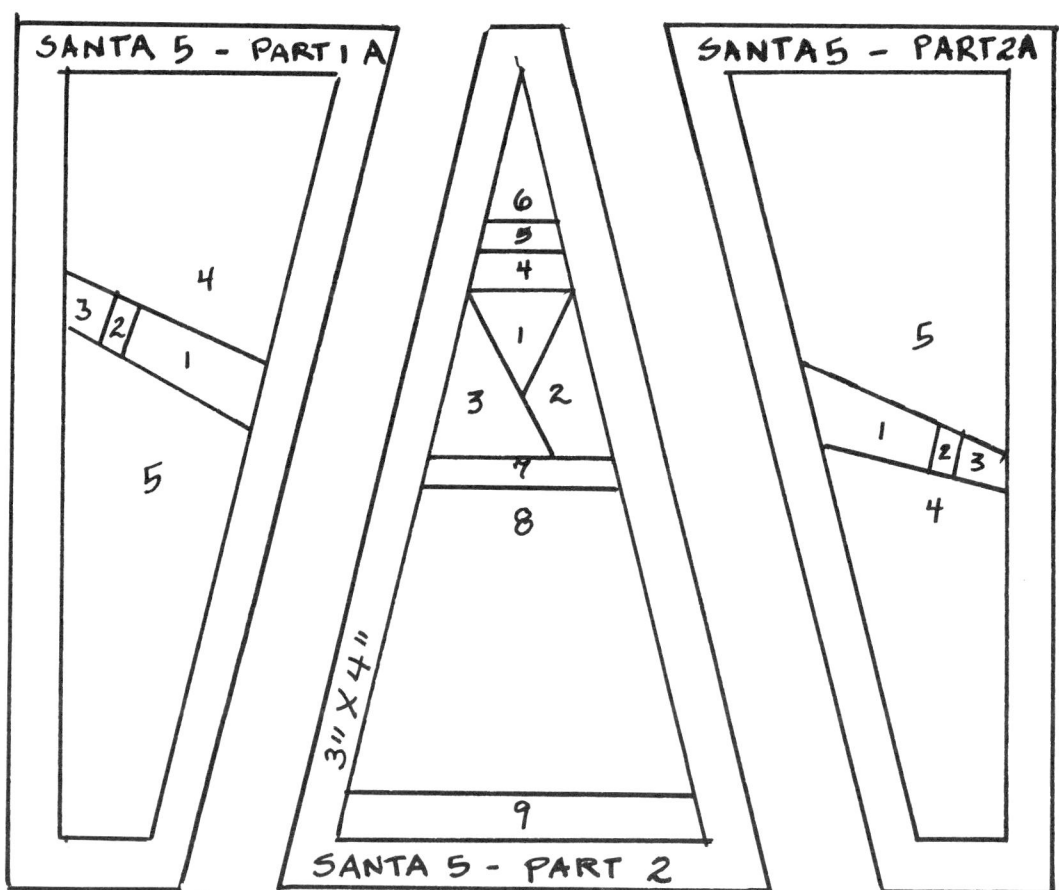

SANTA 5 - PART1A

SANTA 5 - PART2A

SANTA 5 - PART 2

3" X 4"

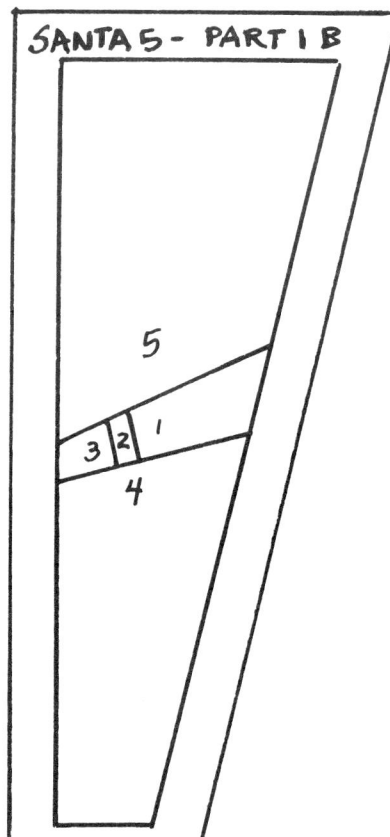

SANTA 5 - PART 1 B

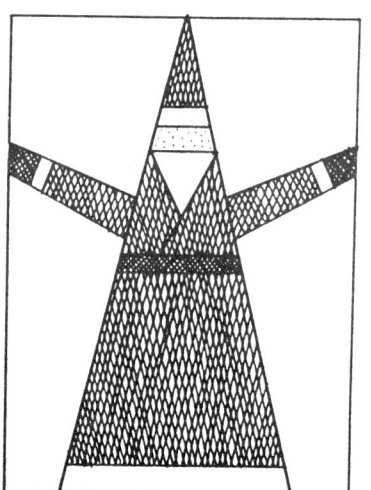

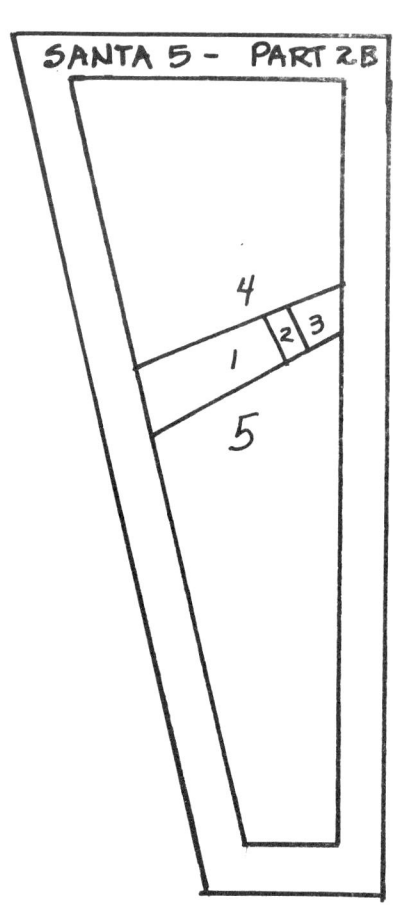

SANTA 5 - PART 2B

Make a whole row of these Santas, with each having different arm positions. This is a mix and match combination that gives you lots of chances to play.

This is a more contemporary Santa. I think he is a lot of fun so I did him facing in both directions so that you can take your pick.

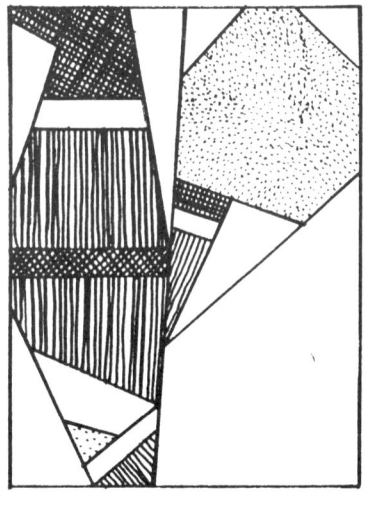

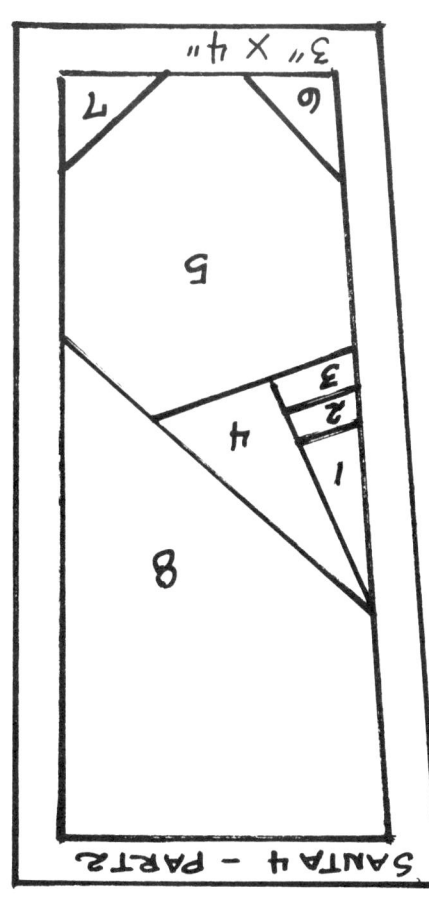

SANTA 4 – PART 2

3" X 4"

SANTA 4 – PART 1

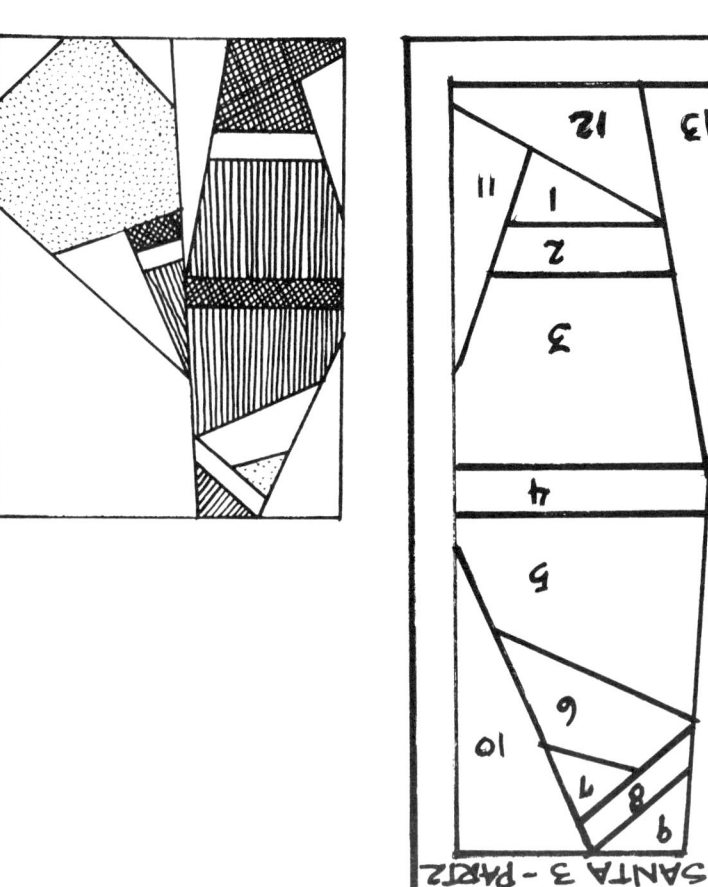

SANTA 3 – PART 2

SANTA 3 – PART 1

3" X 4"

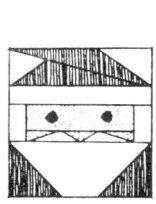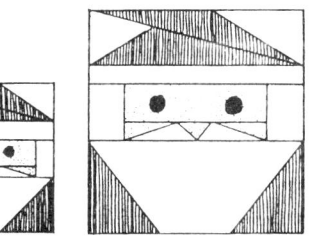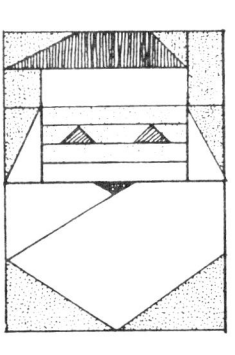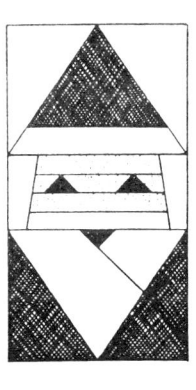

Here are three little Santa faces to play with. One of them needs little beads for eyes. I use little blue wooden beads and put a tiny dot of typing correction fluid on the bead to put that touch of sparkle in his eye. You can add a tiny jingle bell, tassel, or puff ball to the tip of the hat to set the Santa head off.

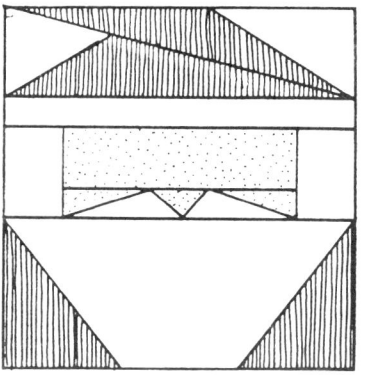

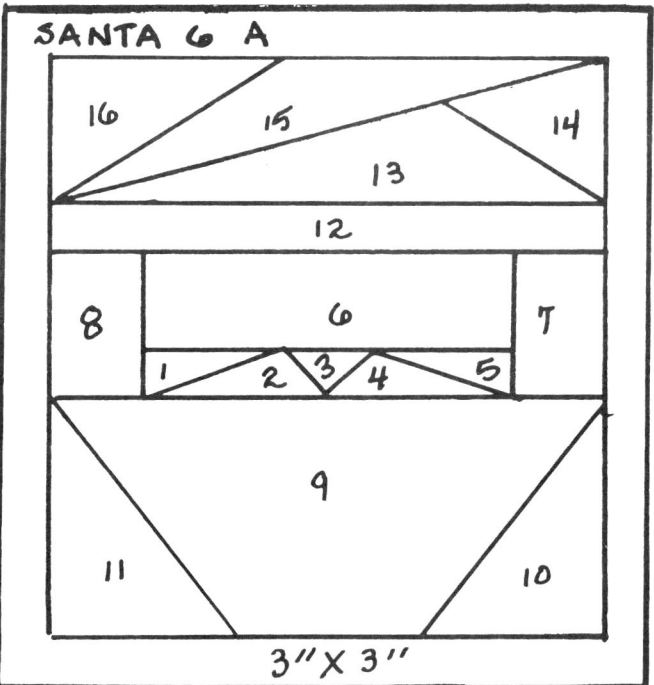

SANTA 6 A

16 15 14
13
12
8 6 7
1 2 3 4 5
9
11 10
3" X 3"

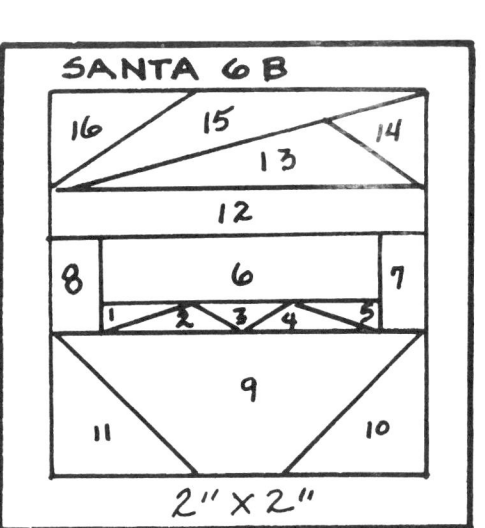

SANTA 6 B

16 15 14
13
12
8 6 7
1 2 3 4 5
9
11 10
2" X 2"

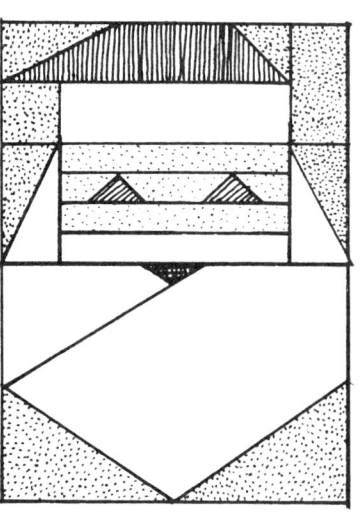

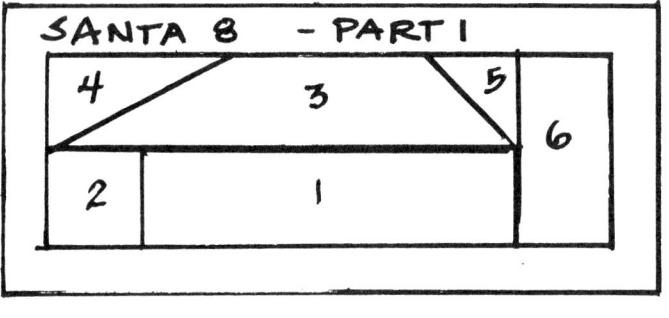

SANTA 8 – PART 1

4 3 5

2 1 6

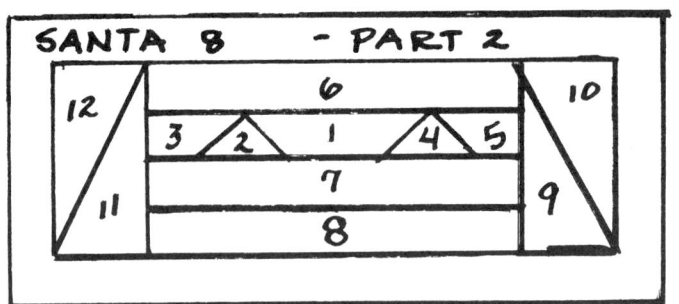

SANTA 8 – PART 2

12 6 10

3 2 1 4 5

11 7 9

8

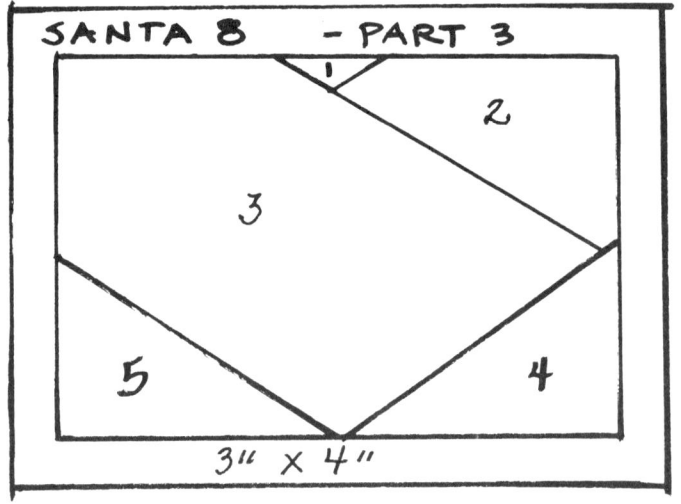

SANTA 8 – PART 3

1 2

3

5 4

3" X 4"

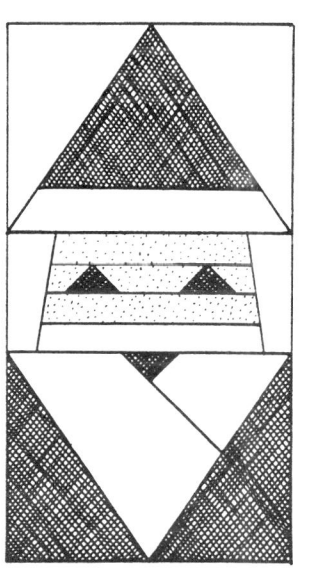

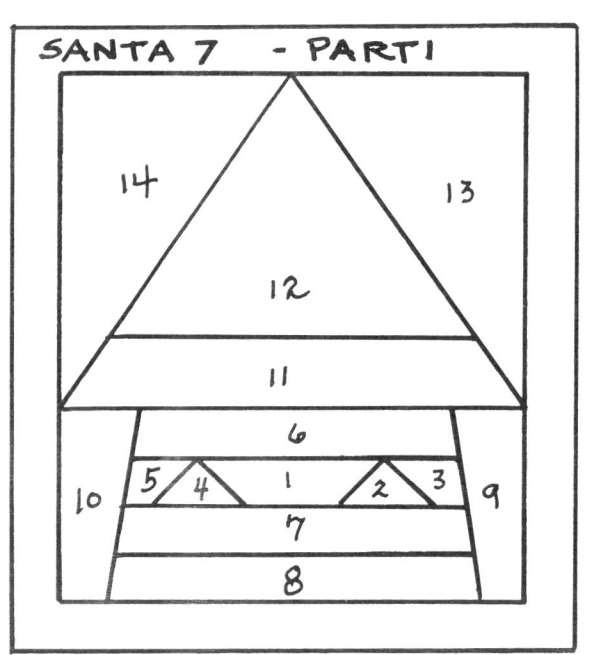

SANTA 7 — PART 1

14   13

12

11

6

10 5 4   1   2 3 9

7

8

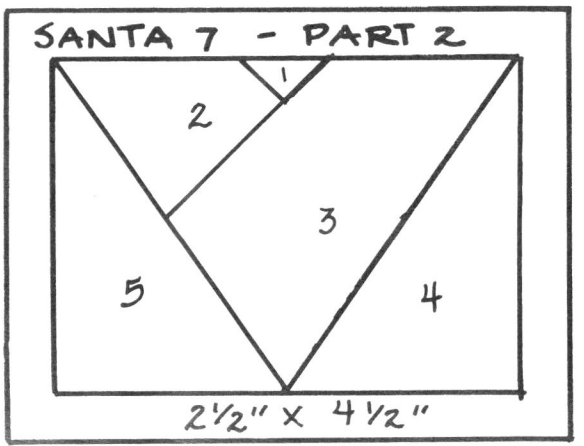

SANTA 7 — PART 2

1

2

3

5   4

2½" X 4½"

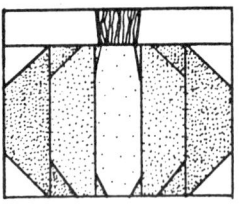
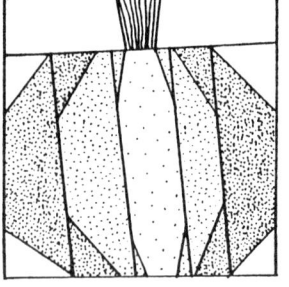
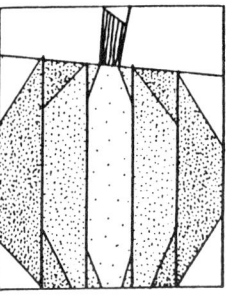
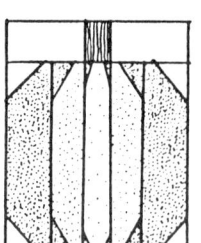

PUMPKINS

Four different pumpkins to choose from and each as cute as can be. Enlarge if you like to make some of those little pieces a little easier to construct.

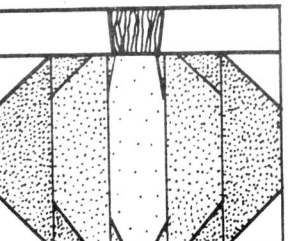

Pumpkin 1 - Part 1

2	1	3

PumpKin 1 - Part 2

16	13	3	2	7	10
15	12	1	6	9	
17	14	4	5	8	11

2½" x 1⅞"

Pump Kin 2 - Part 1

2	1	3

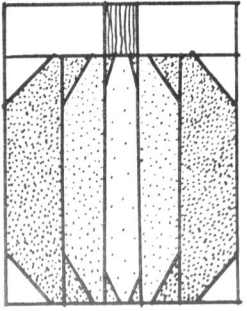

Pumpkin 2   2 3   **Part 2**

16	13			7	10
15	12	1	6	9	
17	14	4 5		8	11

2" X 2½"   4 5

Pumpkin 4 – Part 1

4   2 1   3

Pumpkin – Part 2

16   13   2   3   7   10

15   12   1   6   9

17   14   4   5   8   11

2½" X 3"

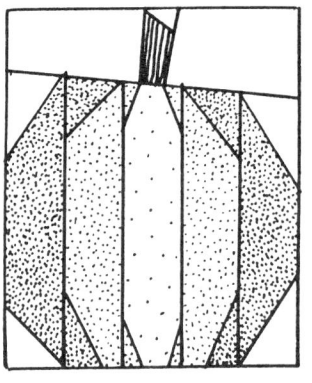

Pumpkin 3 – Part 1

3   1   2

Pumpkin 3   2   3   Part 2

16   13   7   10

15   12   1   6   9

17   14   4   5   8   11

3" X 3"

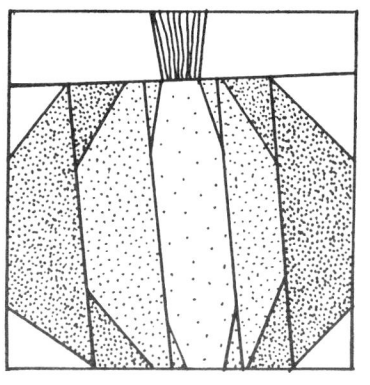

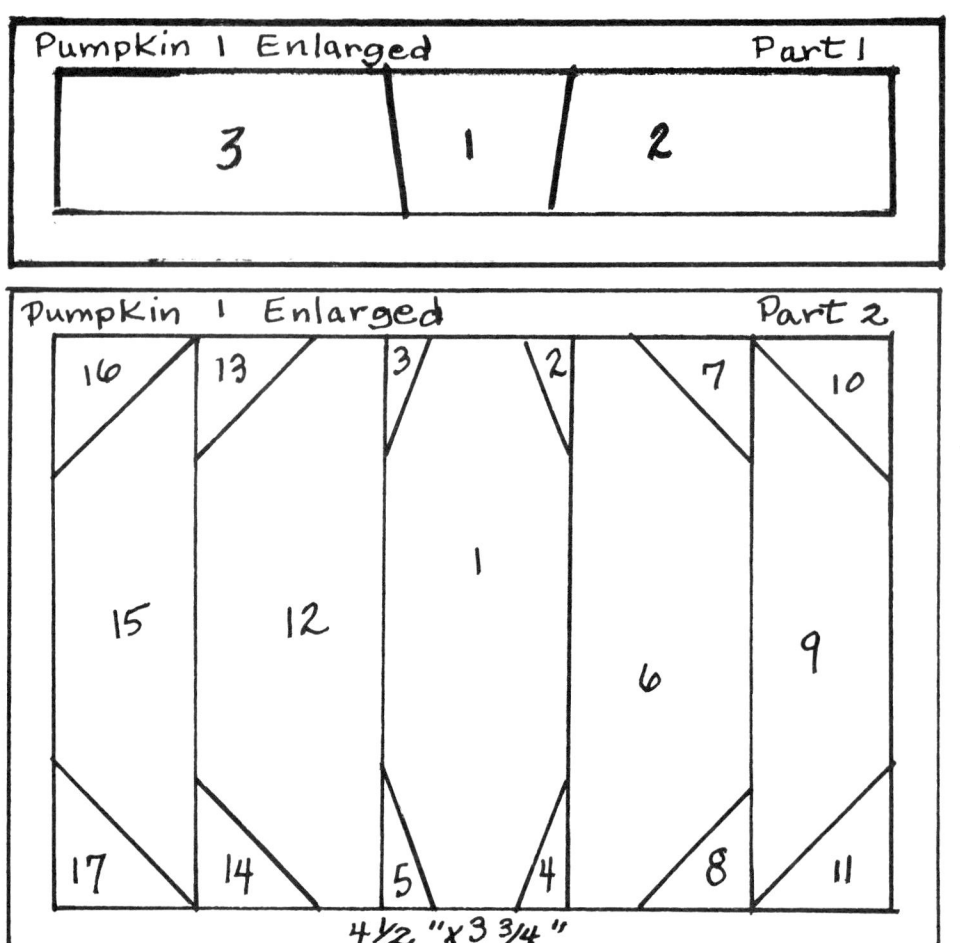

Here is one of the pumpkin designs enlarged for you to try. It is a lot easier to get all of those little pieces in when the design is larger. If you want to enlarge any of the other designs in the book, simply take them to your local copy shop and ask them to enlarge the patterns to whatever size you choose.

WITCH

Here is a simple little witch for you to use with other Halloween designs. There is a small hand design which can be cut from felt and sewn into the seam between piece 4 and piece 5 on each of the arm side parts. Easy and effective, don't you think?

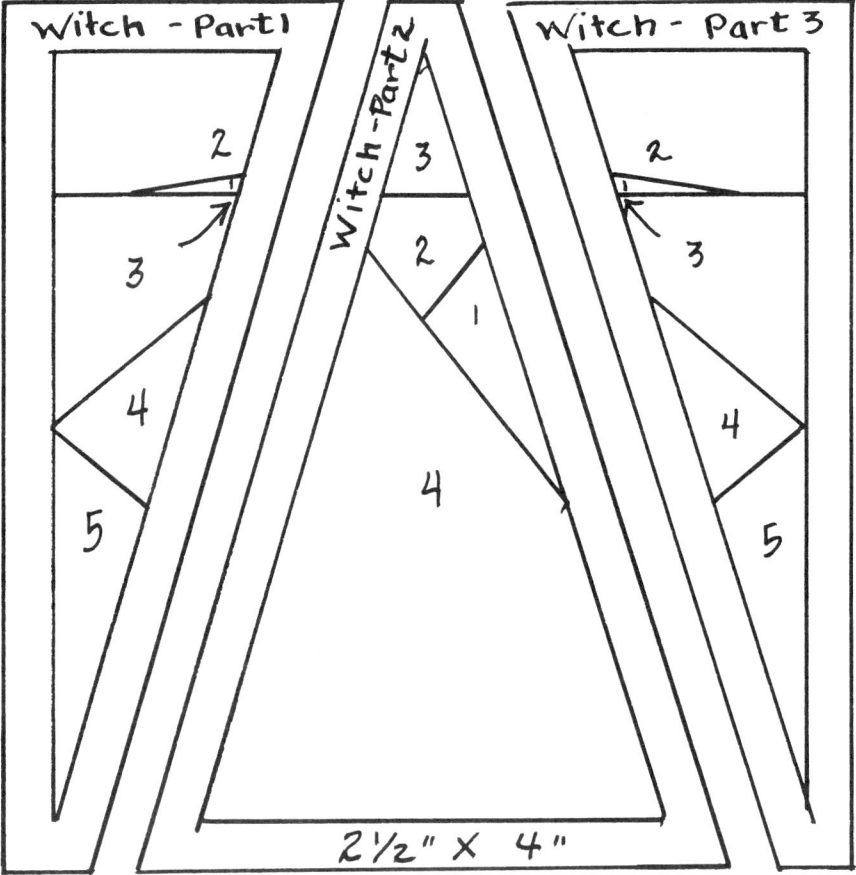

You can add yarn, doll hair, embroidery floss or anything else you can think up to make hair for the witch. Just sew it into the seam between piece 1 (the hat brim) and piece 3. I have placed a little arrow to show you just where to do this. Embroider or draw a mouth and add beads for eyes.

CATS

There are two black cat patterns here. One sits quietly and stares at you and the other arches his back and hisses at you. I have presented them facing both directions so you can pick and choose between them.

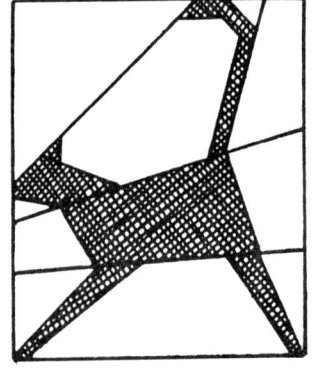

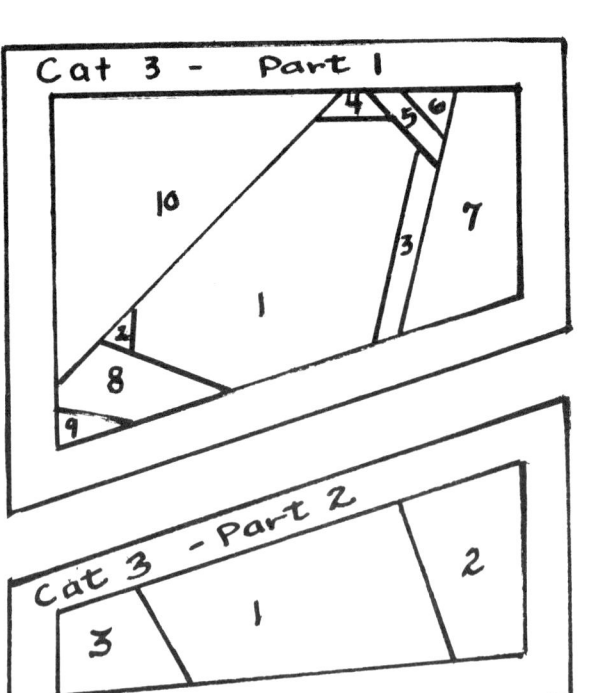

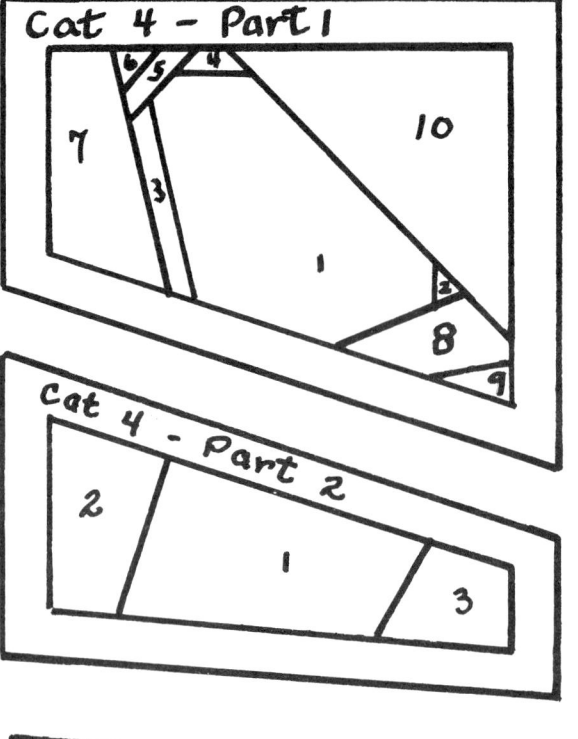

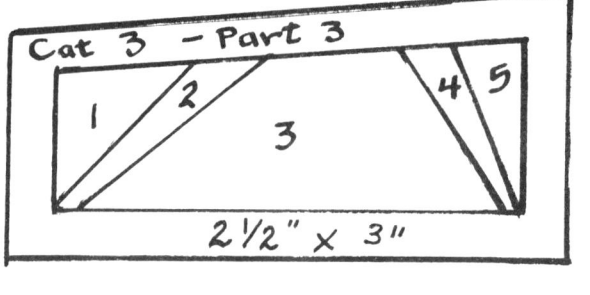

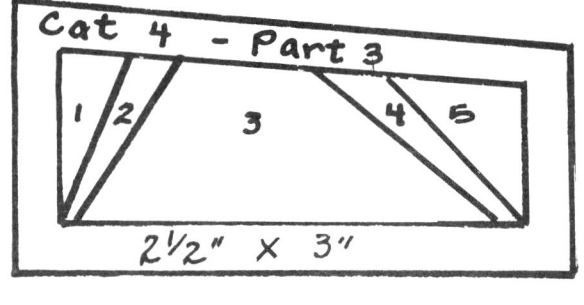

Cat 1 - Part 1

| 1 | 2 | 3 | 4 | 5 |

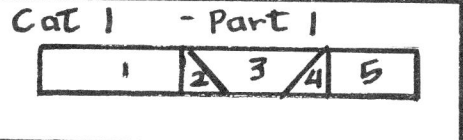

Cat 1 - Part 2

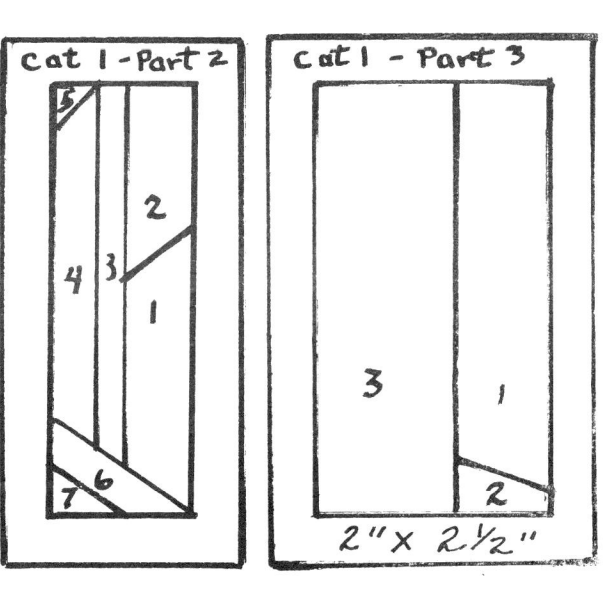

Cat 1 - Part 3

2" X 2½"

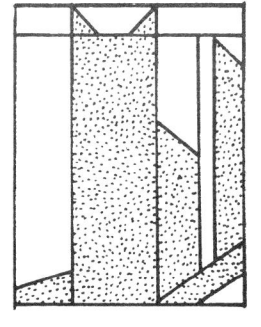

Cat 2 - Part 1

| 3 | 2 | 1 | 4 | 5 |

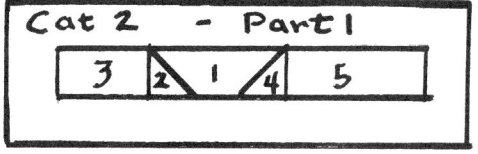

Cat 2 - Part 2

Cat 2 - Part 2

2" X 2½"

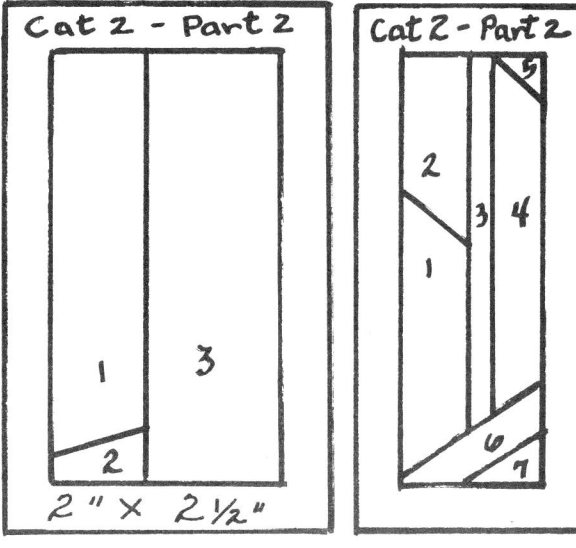

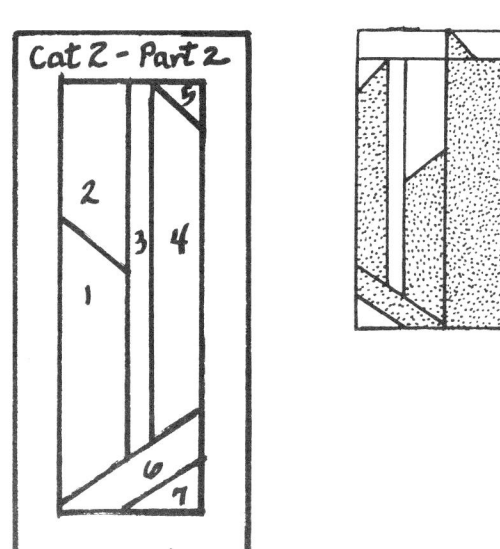

33

HAUNTED HOUSE

The haunted house gives you lots of opportunities to do something really spooky. Maybe you would like to put spooky little faces in the windows. I found a fabric with tiny pumpkins to put in all the windows. Have fun selecting your fabrics!

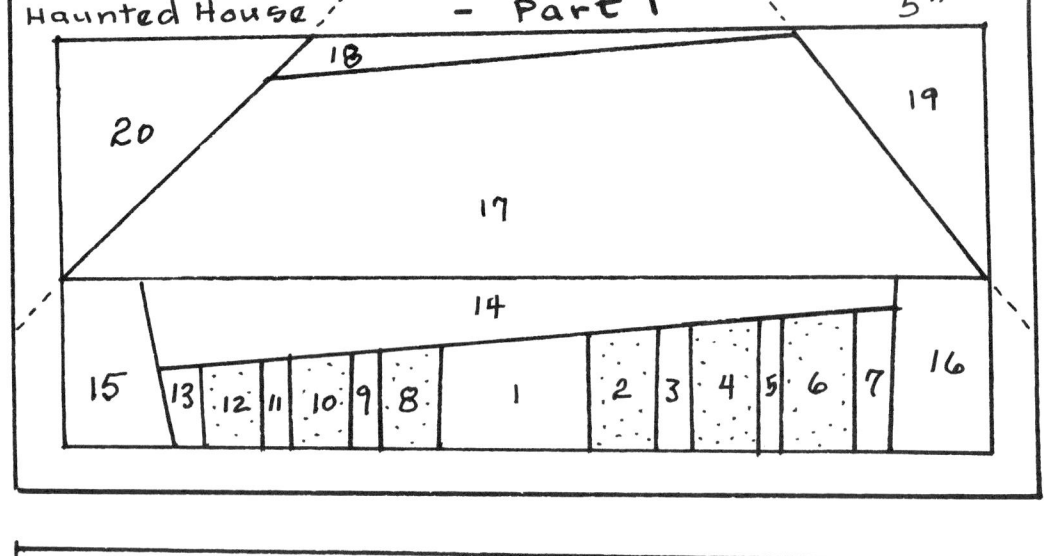

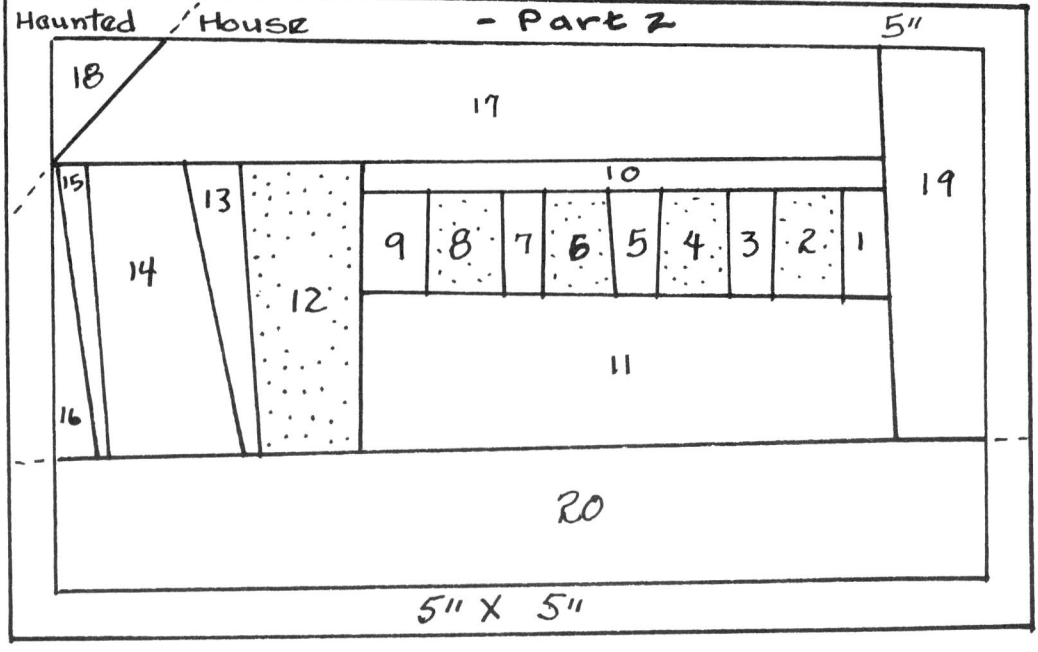

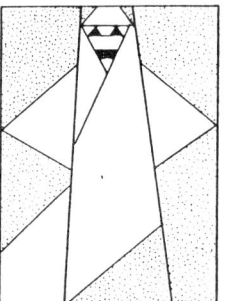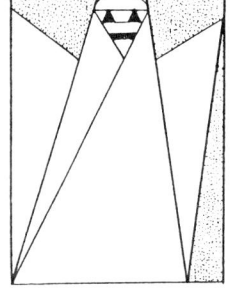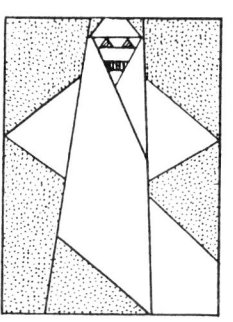

GHOSTS

What color will your ghosts eyes be. I think a bright orange or green might be good. If you don't want to mess with those tiny pieces for the eyes and mouth, simply overlook them when you do the piecing and add beads or French knots for a similar effect.

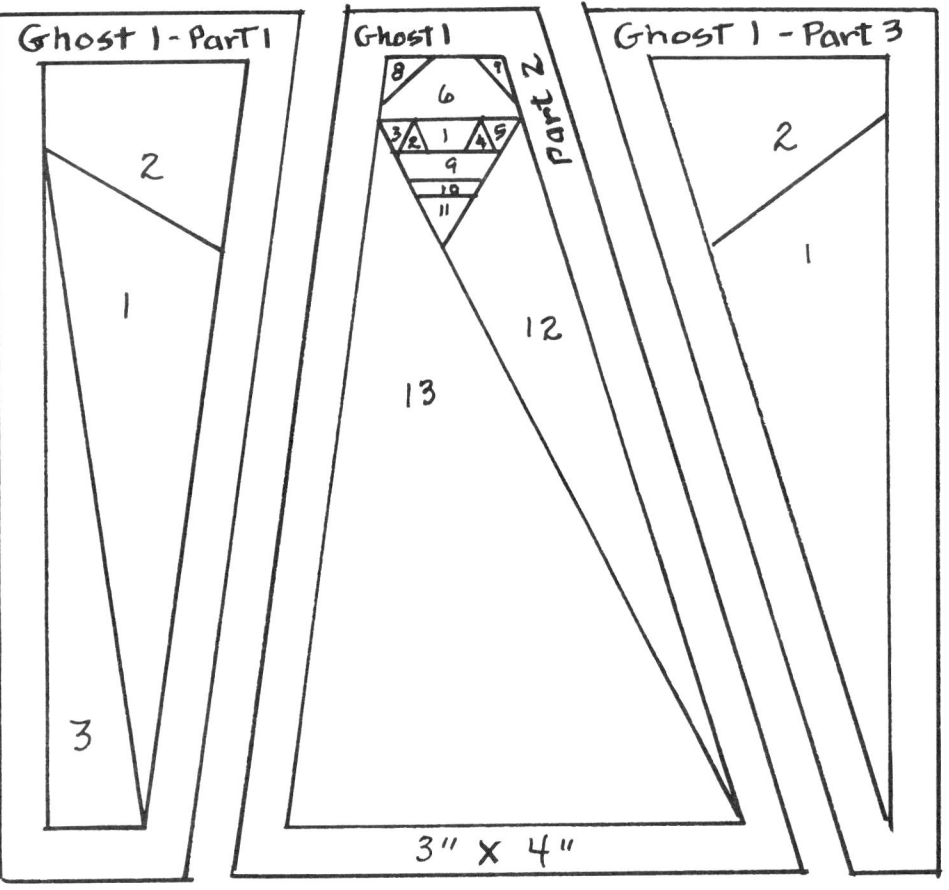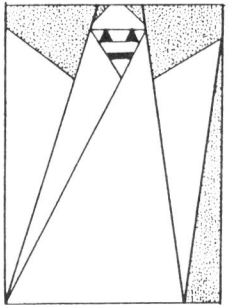

Ghost 1 - Part 1

2

1

3

Ghost 1

8 9
6
3 2 1 4 5
9
10
11

Part 2

12

13

3" x 4"

Ghost 1 - Part 3

2

1

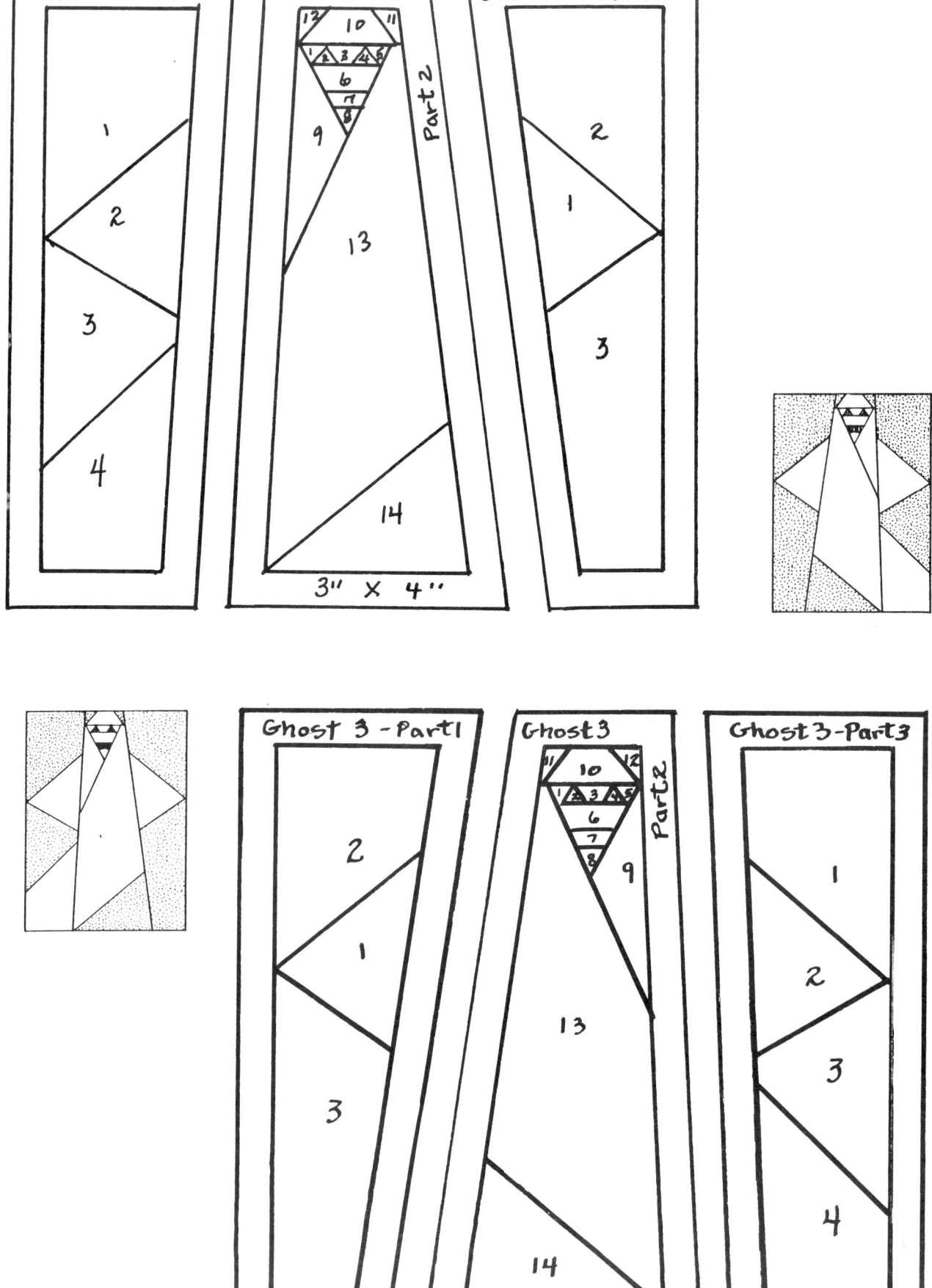

Ghost 2 - Part 1

1
2
3
4

Ghost 2

13
10
11
1 2 3 4 5
6
7
8
9
13
14

3" X 4"

Part 2

Ghost 2 - Part 3

2
1
3

Ghost 3 - Part 1

2
1
3

Ghost 3

11
10
12
1 2 3 4 5
6
7
8
9
13
14

3" X 4"

Part 2

Ghost 3 - Part 3

1
2
3
4

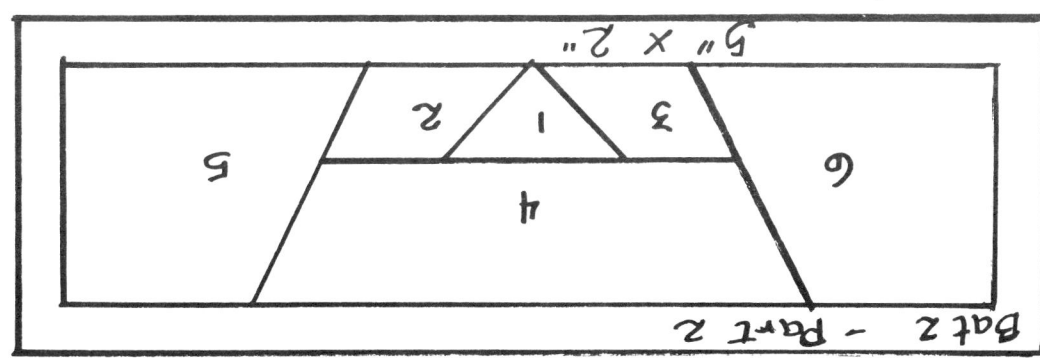

5" x 2"

Bat 2 – Part 2

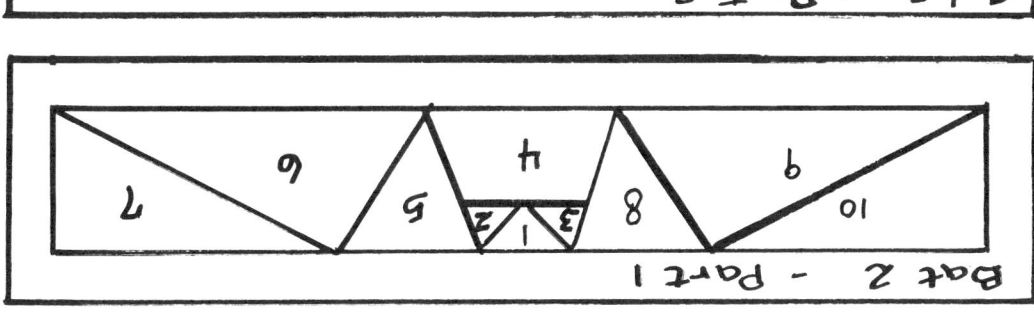

Bat 2 – Part 1

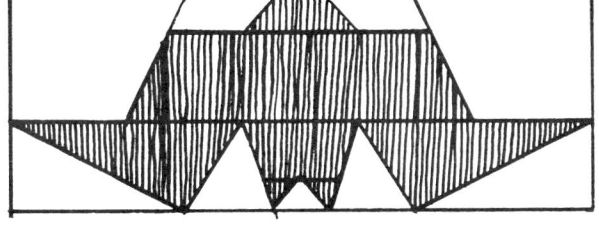

Here are two versions of bats for you to try out. You can slip them into projects as part of the border or flying in the background, barely visible against a dark Halloween sky.

4½" x 1¾"

Bat 1 – Part 2

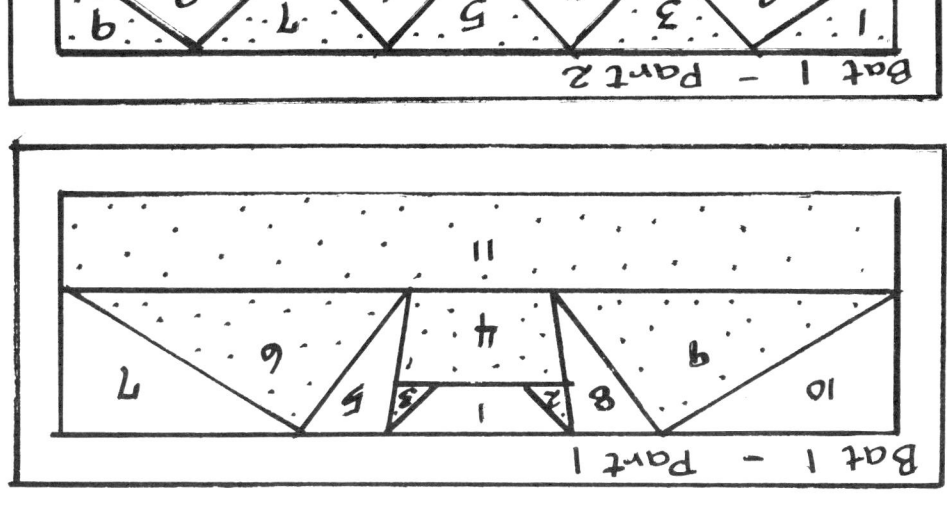

Bat 1 – Part 1

BATS

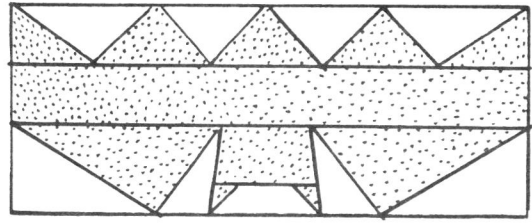

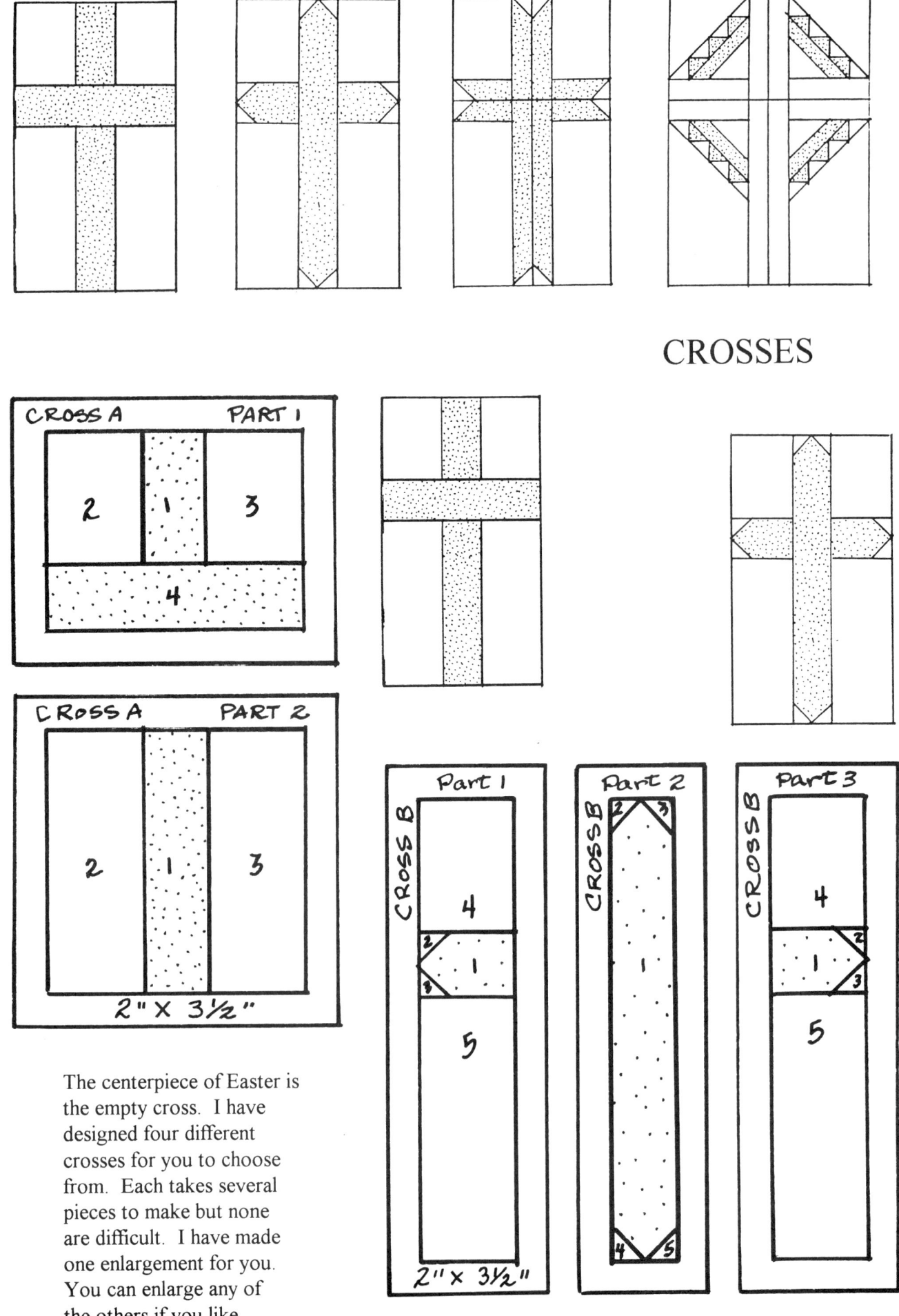

CROSSES

CROSS A   PART 1

2   1   3

4

CROSS A   PART 2

2   1   3

2" X 3½"

The centerpiece of Easter is the empty cross. I have designed four different crosses for you to choose from. Each takes several pieces to make but none are difficult. I have made one enlargement for you. You can enlarge any of the others if you like.

CROSS B   Part 1

4

2
1
3

5

2" X 3½"

CROSS B   Part 2

2   3

1

4   5

CROSS B   Part 3

4

2
1
3

5

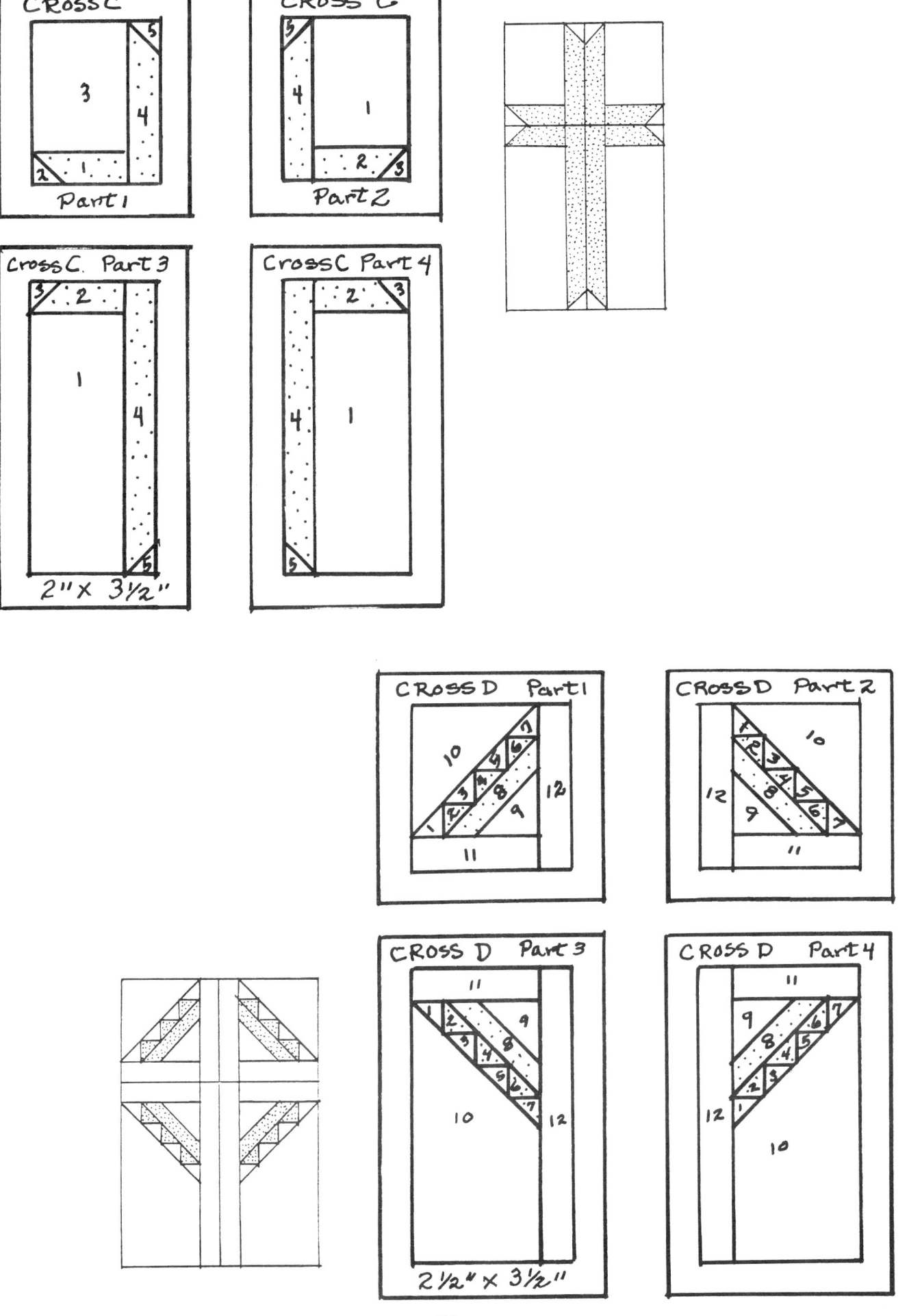

CROSS C Part 1

CROSS C Part 2

CrossC. Part 3

CrossC Part 4

2" x 3½"

CROSS D Part 1

CROSS D Part 2

CROSS D Part 3

2½" x 3½"

CROSS D Part 4

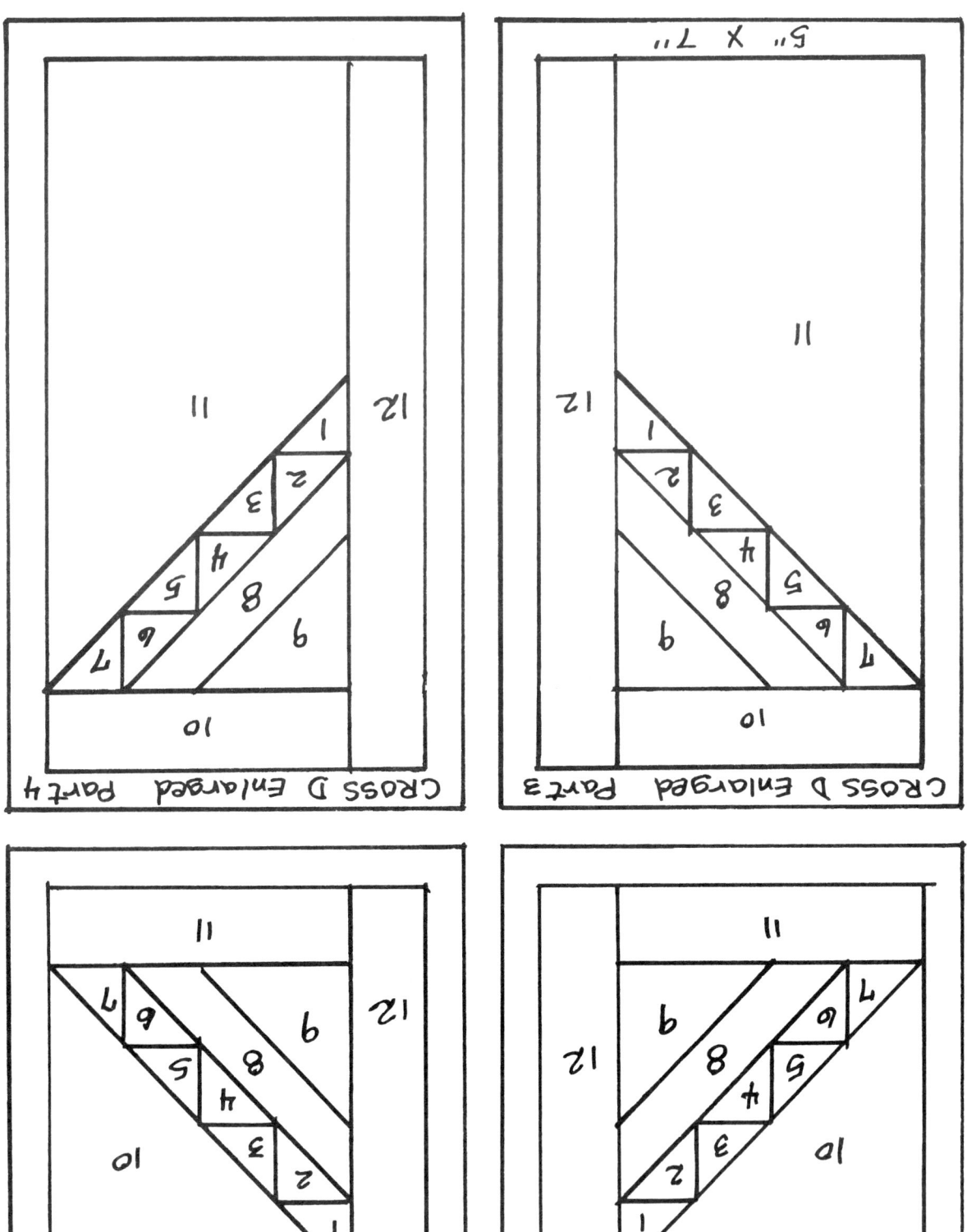

CROSS D Enlarged Part 1

CROSS D Enlarged Part 2

CROSS D Enlarged Part 3

CROSS D Enlarged Part 4

5" X 7"

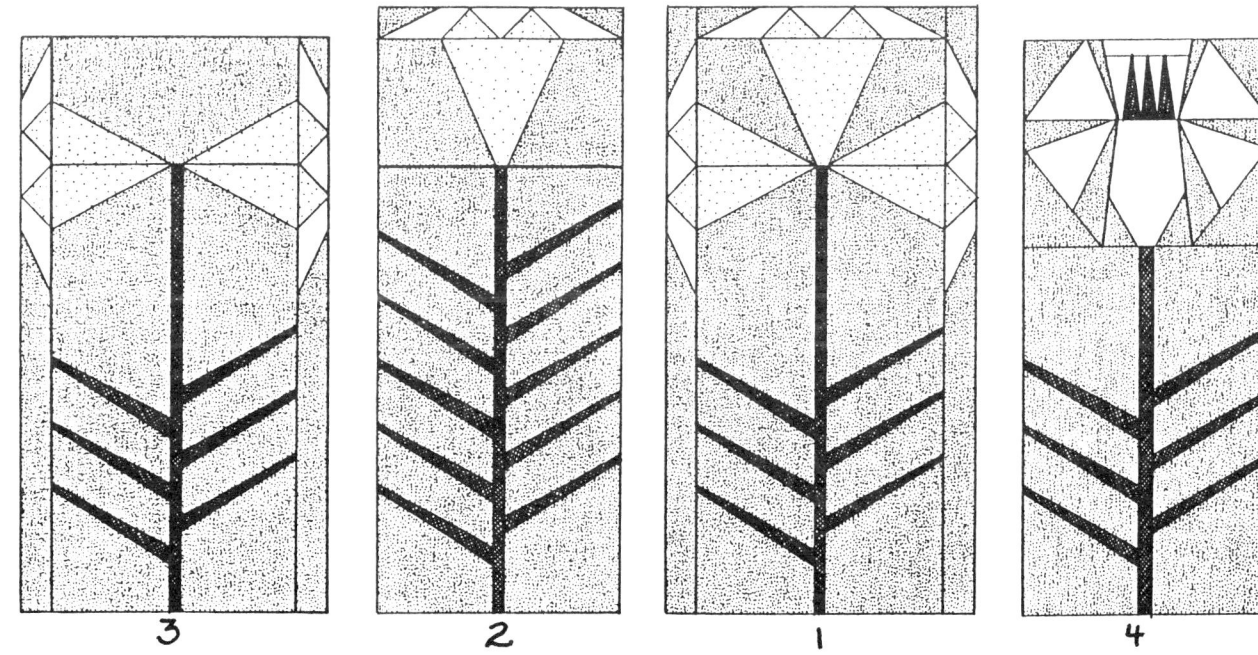

LILIES

What is Easter without the beautiful fragrant white lilies. Here are four different styles to put in your garden. Be sure to look at the block layout for each design so that you construct the proper design with the proper pieces., for there is some duplication of parts. All the parts are easy to assemble, so just take it one part at a time and you will get the job done.

Assembly diagrams and block measurements are on page 47.

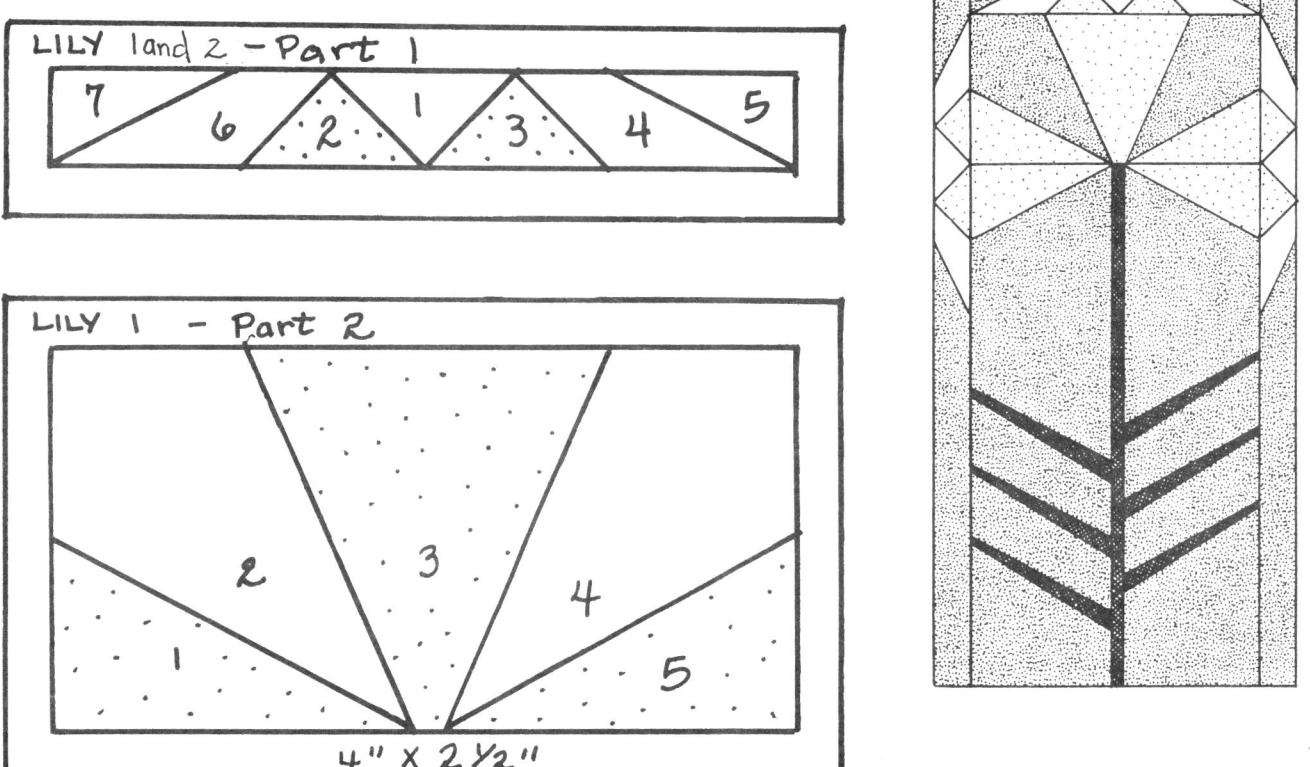

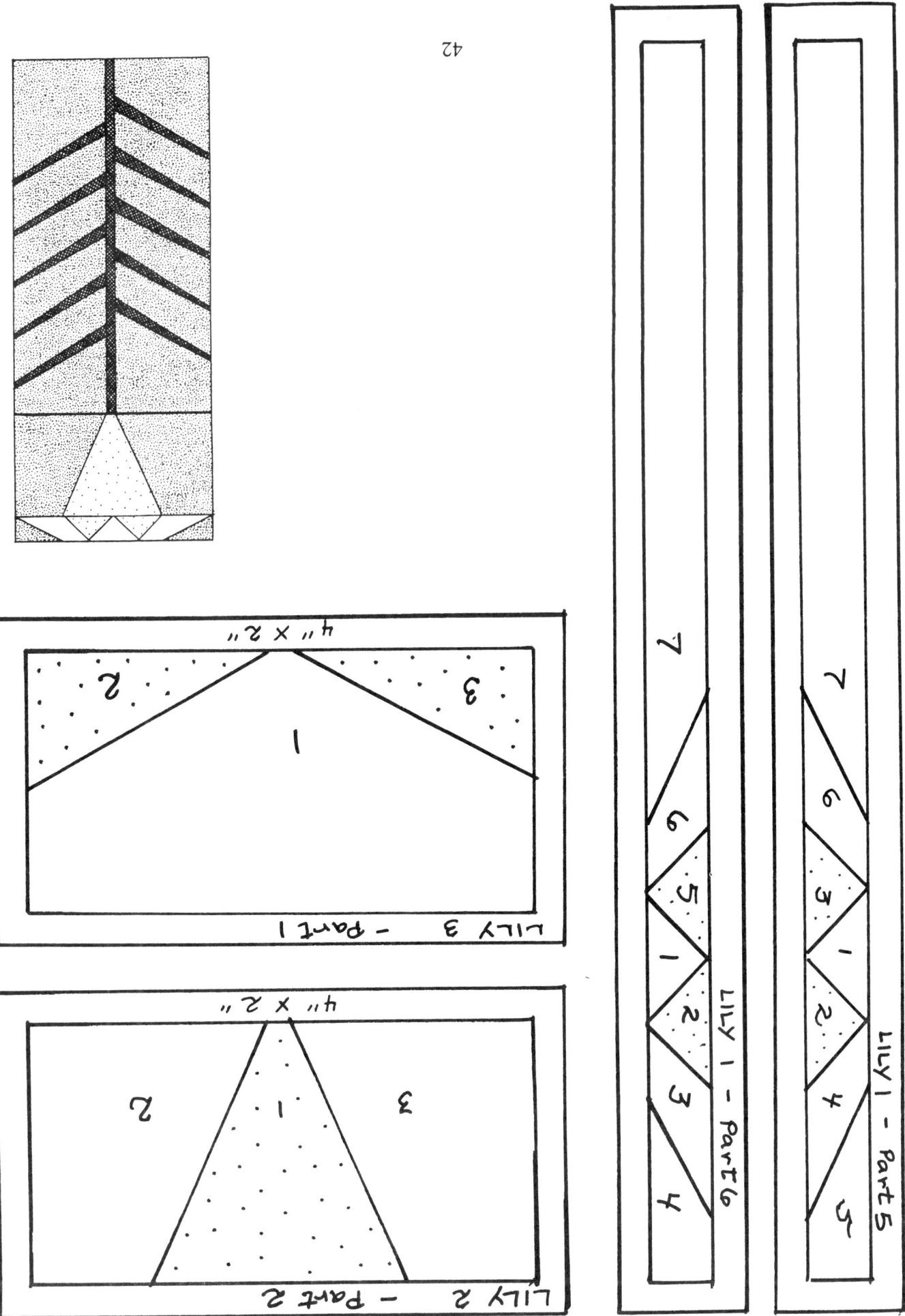

LILY 3 - Part 1

4" x 2"

2

1

3

LILY 2 - Part 2

4" x 2"

2

1

3

LILY 1 - Part 6

7

6

5

1

2

3

4

LILY 1 - Part 5

7

6

3

1

2

4

5

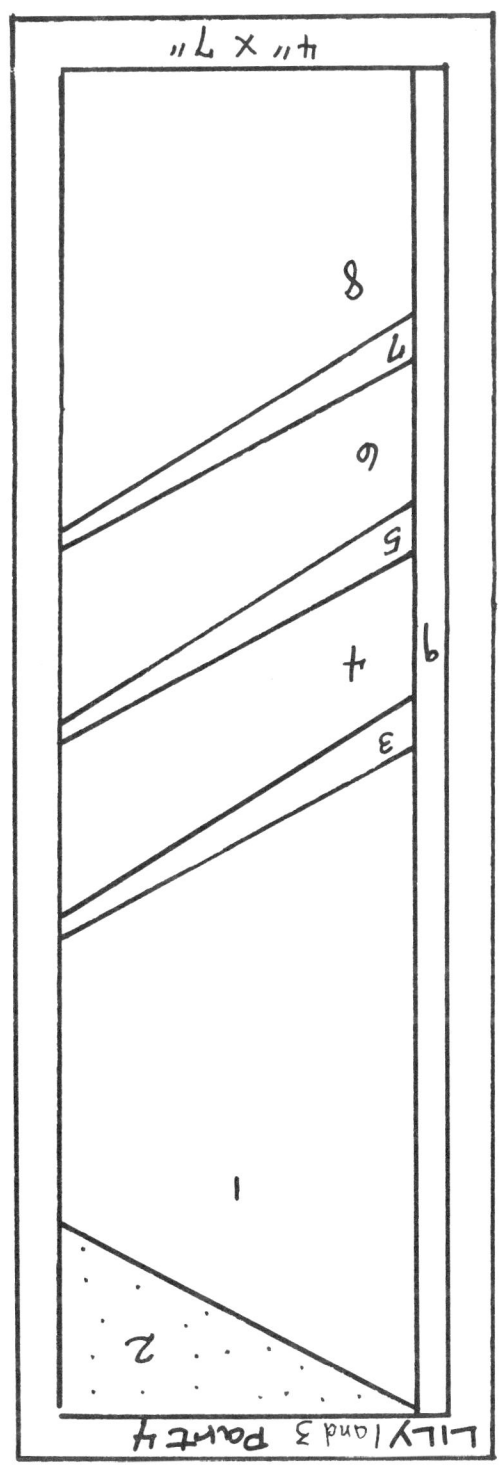

4" x 7"

8
7
6
5
4
3
9
1
2

LILY 1and3 Part 4

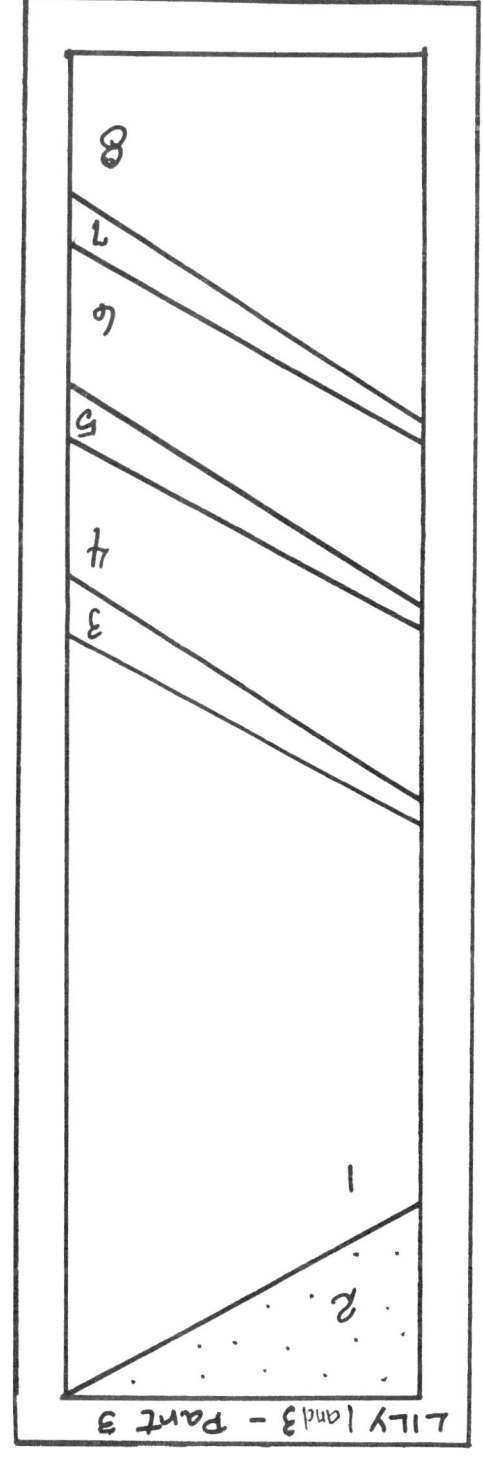

8
7
6
5
4
3
1
2

LILY 1and3 - Part 3

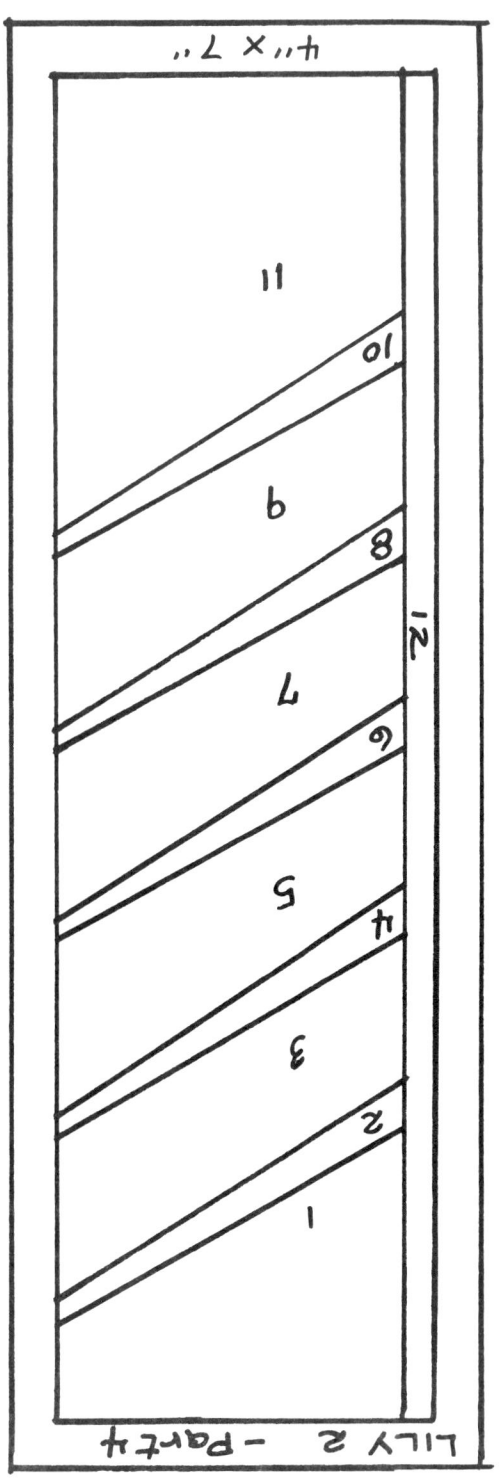

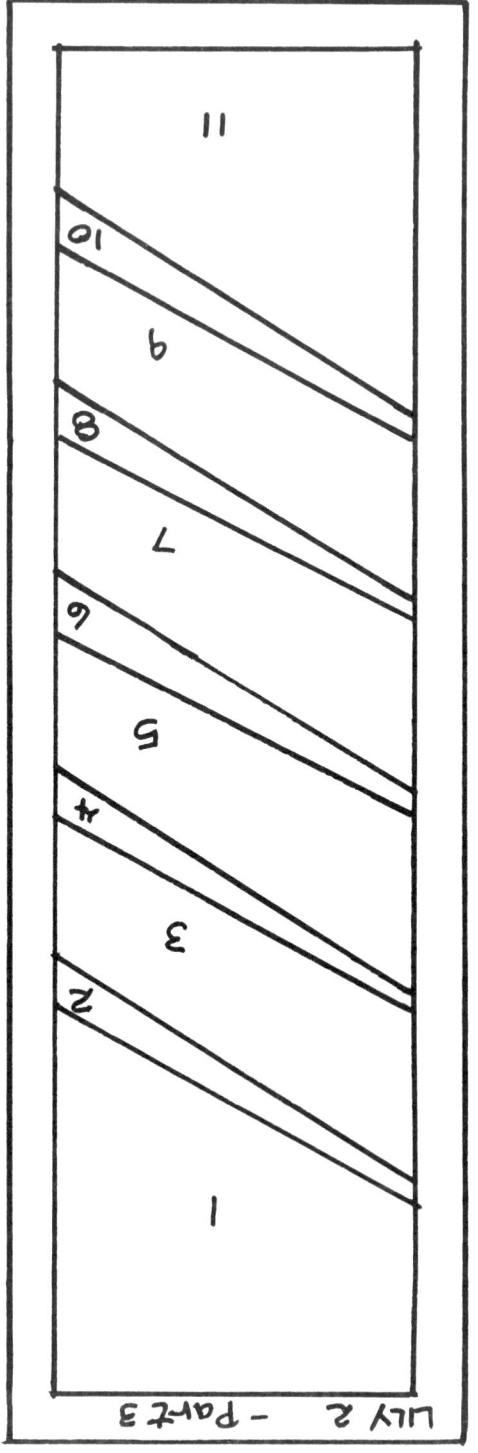

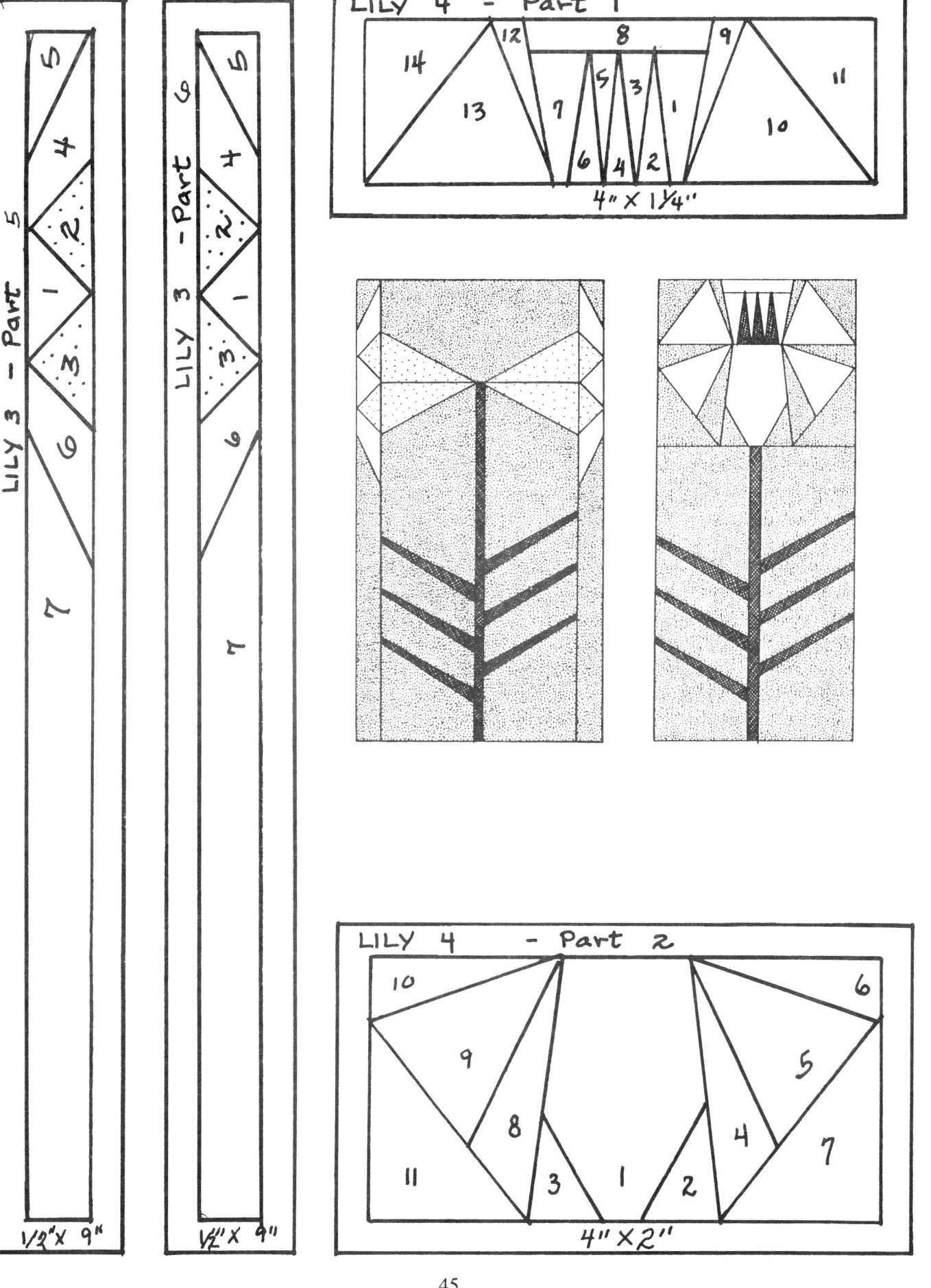

LILY 4 - Part 1

4" × 1¼"

LILY 3 - Part 5

½" × 9"

LILY 3 - Part 6

½" × 9"

LILY 4 - Part 2

4" × 2"

45

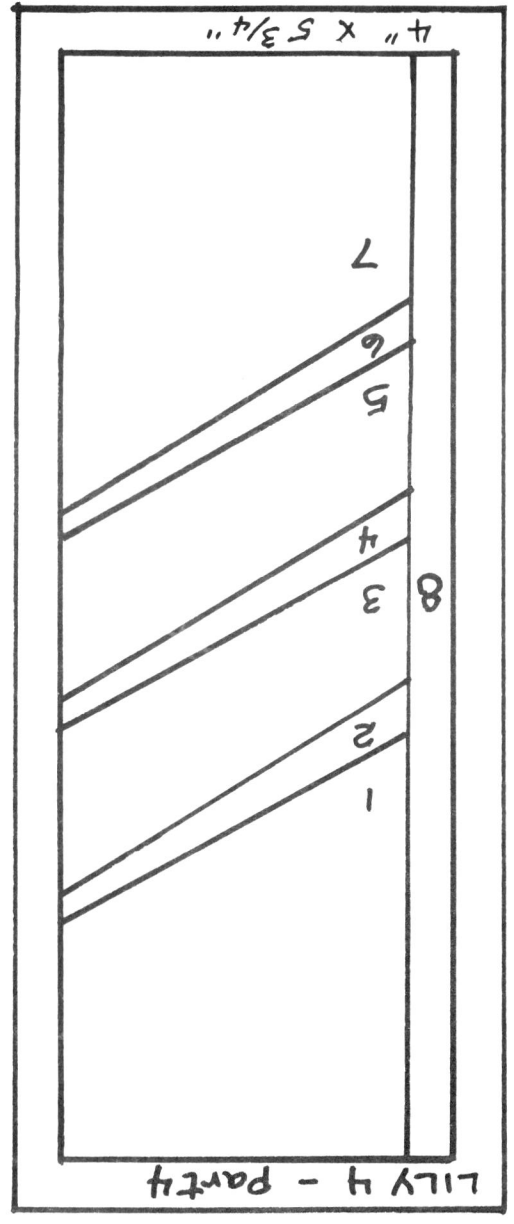

LILY 4 – Part 4

4" x 5 3/4"

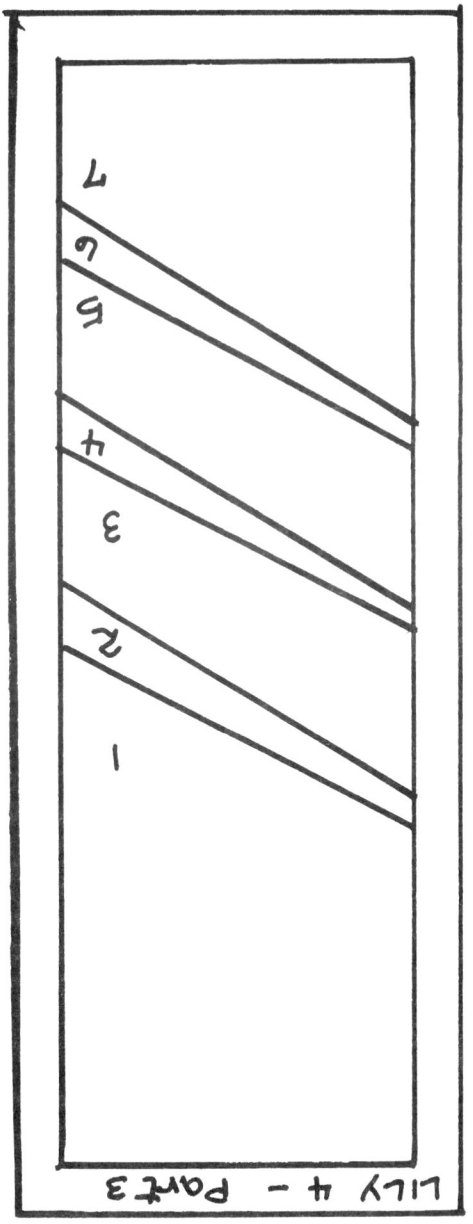

LILY 4 – Part 3

LILY 4 IS 4" X 9"

LILY 3 IS 5" X 9"

LILY 4 PART 4

LILY 4 PART 3

LILY 4 PART 2

LILY 4 PART 1

LILY 3 PART 5

LILY 3 PART 6

LILY 1 PART 4

LILY 1 PART 3

LILY 3 PART 1

LILY 2 IS 4" X 9 1/2"

LILY 1 IS 5" X 9 1/2"

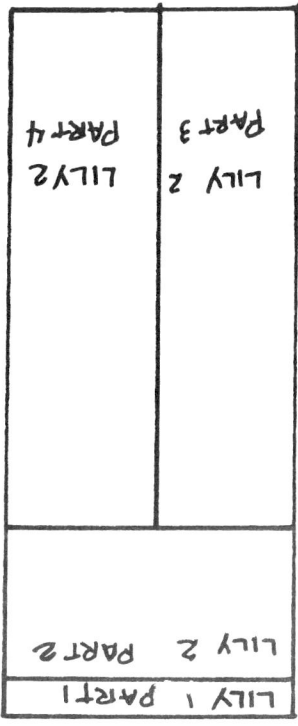

LILY 2 PART 4

LILY 2 PART 3

LILY 2 PART 2

LILY 2 PART 1

LILY 1 PART 5

LILY 1 PART 6

LILY 1 PART 4

LILY 1 PART 3

LILY 1 PART 2

LILY 1 PART 1

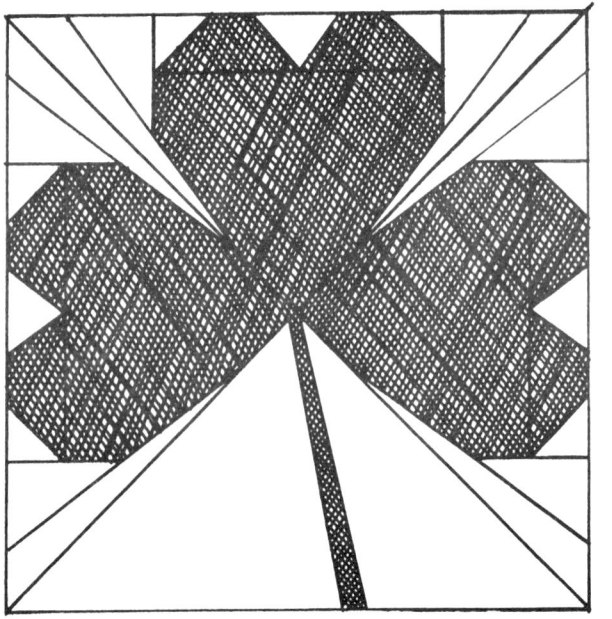

SHAMROCK

The shamrock is the most frequent symbol for St. Patrick's day every March the 17th. Two easy pattern pieces will do the trick. If you want to make a fun scrap quilt using hearts, try making four units with the heart motif and put them together.

HEARTS

The shamrock is made with three heart shaped pieces which make a nice design for Valentine's Day. Simply make four pieces instead of three.

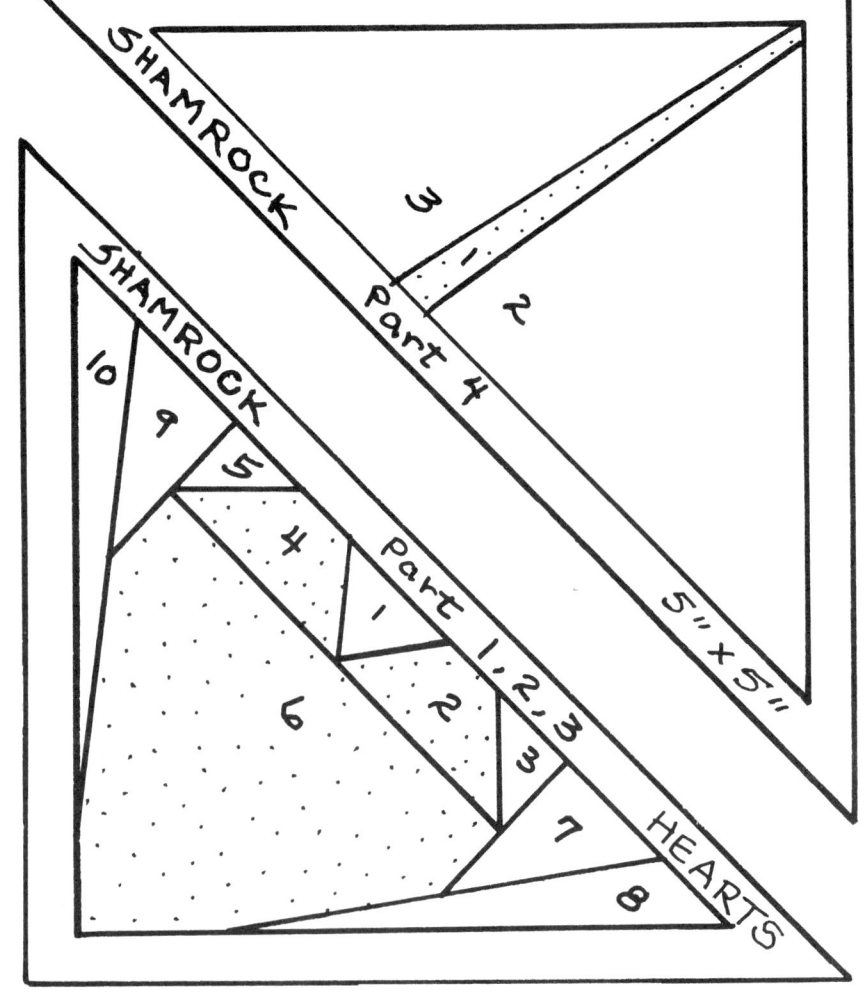

FIREWORKS

Everyone gets into the spirit of the holiday when we go to the local fireworks on the 4th! I have included stripes on the fire crackers and rockets but you can make them plain colors by simply ignoring the little stripe sections.

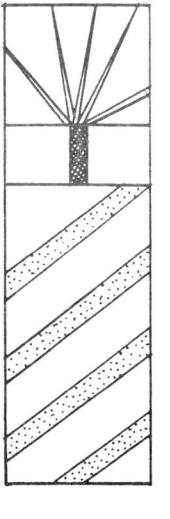
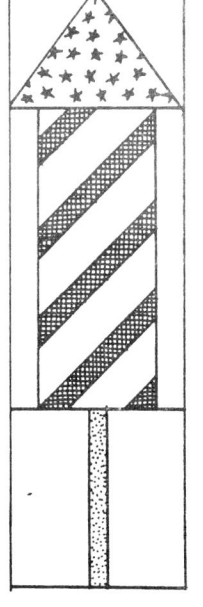

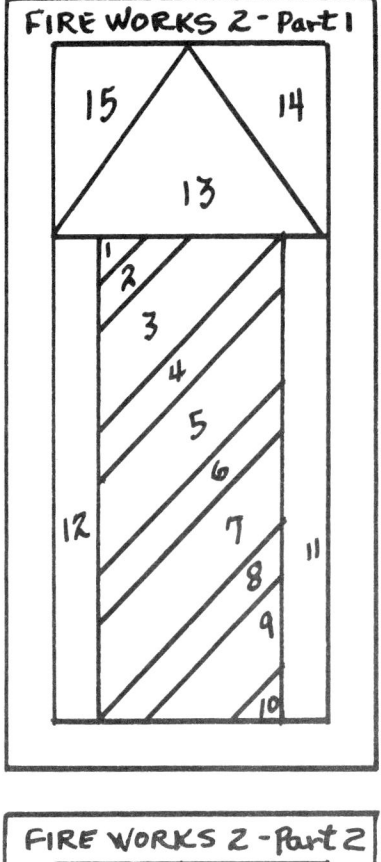

FIRE WORKS 2 - Part 1

15 14
13
1
2
3
4
5
6
12   7   11
8
9
10

FIRE WORKS 1 Part 1

8 6 4
7 5 3
9   →2
10
11   1

FIRE WORKS 1 Part 2

3 | 1 | 2

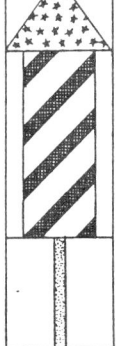

FIRE WORKS 2 - Part 2

3 | 1 | 2

1½" x 5"

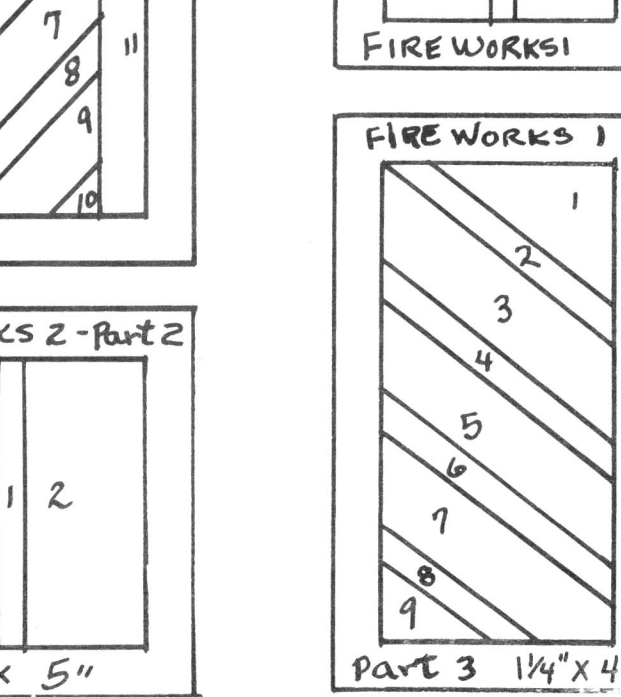

FIRE WORKS 1

1
2
3
4
5
6
7
8
9

Part 3   1¼" x 4"

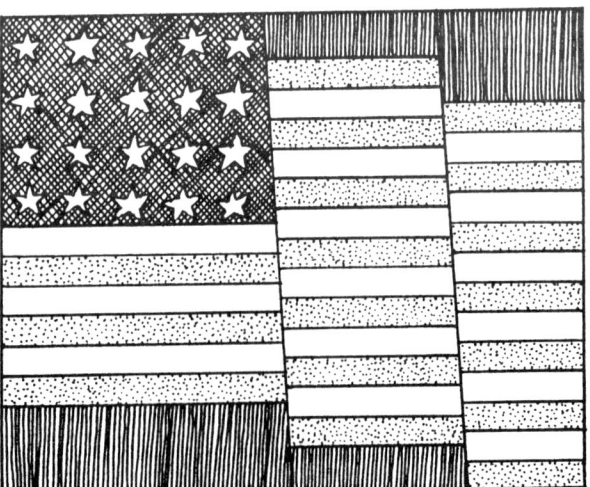

AMERICAN FLAG

The American flag is the symbol of liberty to much of the world today. Use a blue fabric with tiny stars for the section one on pattern piece three. You can add a flag pole to this pattern if you like.

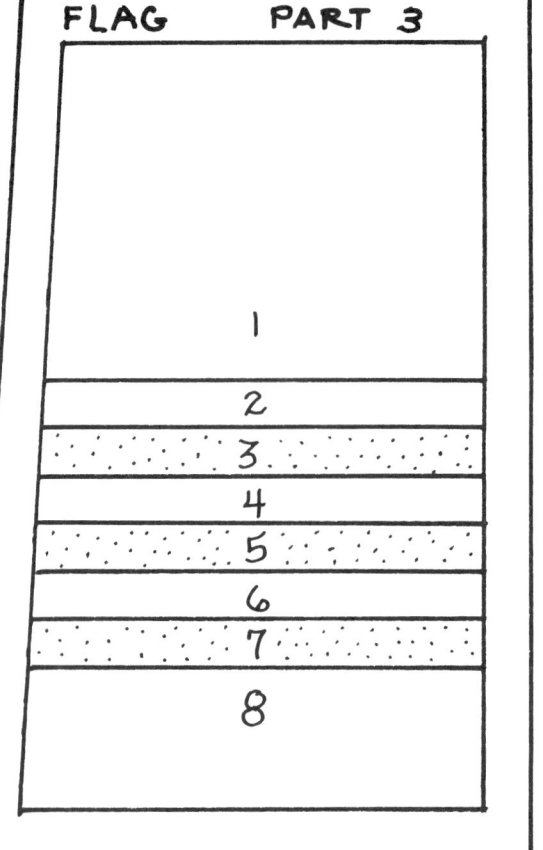

FLAG PART 1
1
2
3
4
5
6
7
8
9
10
11
12
13
14

FLAG PART 2
1
2
3
4
5
6
7
8
9
10
11
12
13
14
15

5" X 4"

FLAG PART 3
1
2
3
4
5
6
7
8

EAGLE

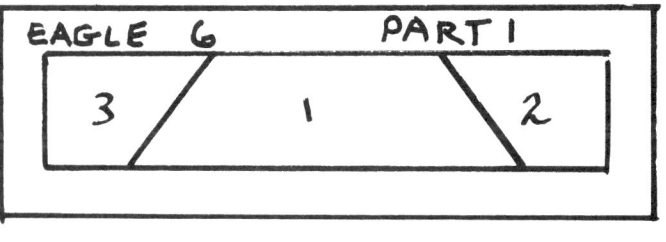

Here is a very stylized eagle head to add to the patriotic designs. Give him a red, white and blue treatment or make him in natural coloring.

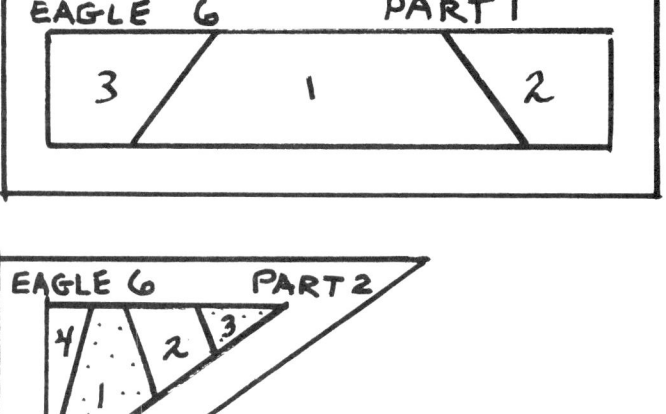

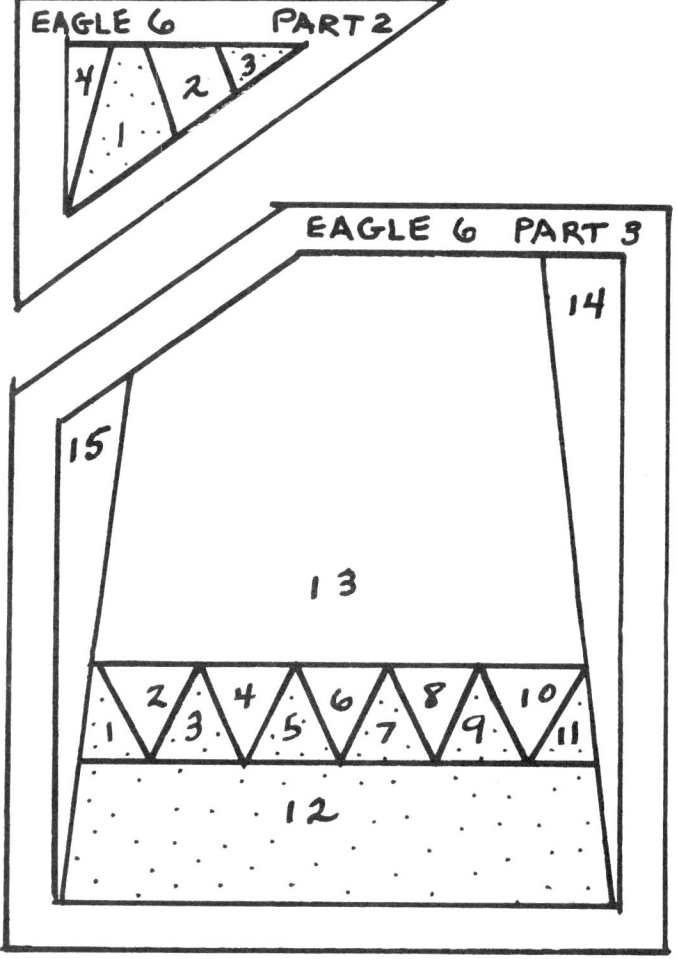